Emotional Intelligence

ACHIEVING ACADEMIC AND CAREER EXCELLENCE

SECOND EDITION

Darwin B. Nelson

TEXAS A&M UNIVERSITY—KINGSVILLE

Gary R. Low

TEXAS A&M UNIVERSITY—KINGSVILLE

Prentice Hall

Boston   Columbus   Indianapolis   New York   San Francisco   Upper Saddle River
Amsterdam   Cape Town   Dubai   London   Madrid   Milan   Munich   Paris   Montreal   Toronto
Delhi   Mexico City   Sao Paulo   Sydney   Hong Kong   Seoul   Singapore   Taipei   Tokyo

Executive Editor: Sande Johnson
Editorial Assistant: Clara Ciminelli
Vice President, Director of Marketing: Quinn Perkson
Executive Marketing Manager: Amy Judd
Marketing Assistant: Robin Holtsberry
Production Editor: Cynthia Parsons
Project Manager: Susan Hannahs
Senior Art Director: Jayne Conte

Cover Designer: Suzanne Behnke
Cover Art: Getty Images, Inc.
Full-Service Project Management: Jogender Taneja/ Aptara®, Inc.
Composition: Aptara®, Inc.
Printer/Bindery: RR Donnelley/Crawfordsville
Text Font: GoudyWtcTReg

Credits and acknowledgments borrowed from other sources and reproduced, with permission, in this textbook appear on appropriate page within the text.

Photo Credits: Stanislav Popov/Shutterstock, p. xxiii; Denis Vrublevski/Shutterstock, p. 1; Pattie Steib/Shutterstock, p. 17; Jupiter Unlimited, p. 41; Chris Schmidt/iStockphoto, p. 73; Stephen Coburn/Shutterstock, p. 101; Phase4Photography/Shutterstock, p. 135; Mike Norton/Shutterstock, p. 141; Andresr/Shutterstock, p. 165.

Every effort has been made to provide accurate and current Internet information in this book. However, the Internet and information posted on it are constantly changing, so it is inevitable that some of the Internet addresses listed in this textbook will change.

Many of the designations by manufacturers and seller to distinguish their products are claimed as trademarks. Where those designations appear in this book, and the publisher was aware of a trademark claim, the designations have been printed in initial caps or all caps.

Library of Congress Cataloging-in-Publication Data

Nelson, Darwin B.
  Emotional intelligence : achieving academic and career excellence in college and life / Darwin B. Nelson, Gary R. Low.—2nd ed.
    p. cm.
  Includes bibliographical references and index.
  ISBN-13: 978-0-13-502299-3
  ISBN-10: 0-13-502299-1
  1. College students—Life skills guides. 2. College student orientation. 3. Emotional intelligence. 4. Interpersonal relations. I. Low, Gary R. II. Title.
  LB2343.3.N45 2011
  378.1′98—dc22

                                                                                        2009050841

10 9 8 7 6 5 4 3 2 1

Prentice Hall
is an imprint of

www.pearsonhighered.com

ISBN 13: 978-0-13-502299-3
ISBN 10:   0-13-502299-1

DEDICATION

Emotional Intelligence: Achieving Academic and Career Excellence is dedicated to new and first-generation college students everywhere making the important and challenging transition from home to school to college to career. These students have inspired us to develop the best book and learning system possible to help guide them on their way to personal excellence.

Through research, teaching, learning, and life experiences, we have learned that emotional intelligence (EI) is the most important factor in college, career, and life success. This expanded preface highlights several concepts important to our work and the second edition. This new edition highlights research-derived applications and people who use our EI assessments and learning systems in exemplary ways, including colleges and organizations. Our annual Institute for Emotional Intelligence provides a forum for sharing and learning about the emerging theory of EI and our education models. A link to our Web site with information about the annual conference is provided in the preface. More than ever before, our focus is on the direct connection between EI skills and strategies for achieving teaching, learning, leadership and life excellence.

Students will see references to a fictional character, *EI Man*, in exhibits throughout the book. Although not illustrated, we created *EI Man* to provide a wise and caring mentor/guide who understands the importance of emotional intelligence for achievement, career success, and life excellence. We envisioned *EI Man* as a caring mentor with practical wisdom to share the many positive contributions of the emotional mind and EI skills for students everywhere. We hope that caring and dedicated teachers and mentors inspire all students to learn the skills, behaviors, and attitudes of emotional intelligence.

BRIEF CONTENTS

CONTENTS

5 SELF-MANAGEMENT SKILLS   101

Drive Strength, Commitment Ethic, Time Management, and Positive Change   101

6 INTRAPERSONAL SKILLS   135

Self-Esteem and Stress Management   135

Emotional Intelligence: Achieving Academic and Career Excellence is an engaging and self-directed guide for you to learn the contributions of your emotional mind. The purpose of the book is to help you explore, identify, understand, learn, and apply emotional skills essential to your academic and career success. You will learn about emotional intelligence and its importance to achievement, college success, career direction, and leadership. Even more important, you can learn to become as successful as you choose by learning, developing, and applying EI skills and behaviors.

The second edition keeps its focus on you as a person embarking on an important part of your life. You are the most valuable resource in our society. Our goal is to share information, a learning process, and skills that will guide your transition from school to college to career. Emotional Intelligence is a learned ability to think constructively and act wisely.

As you read and engage yourself with EI lessons, you will be learning in ways that you enjoy. Discovering information about yourself and then learning new skills is exciting, enjoyable, and highly productive. In this second edition of *Emotional Intelligence: Achieving Academic and Career Excellence*, you will learn:

- Hallmarks of Excellence for you as a goal-achieving student and person
- Awareness of your own skills and areas to improve with the ESAP
- College and life success skills that are new to you
- Excellence is self-defined and self-directed
- Ten EI skills for academic, career, and everyday life success by following the Emotional Learning System
- Three potential problem areas for many people and corrective strategies
- Five key skills for college success through the Intelligent Self-Direction section of the book
- Practical ways to think reflectively and set goals for achievement
- Contributions of emotional skills and your emotional mind
- The value of self-assessment to manage stress and change

WHAT'S NEW IN THIS EDITION

- **"Hallmarks of Excellence" feature** provides students with theory-based and research-derived information about how the brain works in regard to emotional intelligence and practical emotional learning.

- **A focus on intelligent self-direction** lends a clear focus to the five most important skills for academic excellence: assertion, time management, personal responsibility, drive strength, and stress management.

- **Illustrations and personal narratives** located at the end of each chapter make learning more personally meaningful and less traditional while identifying the contributions of the emotional mind.

- **New findings from adolescent and adult neuroscience** showing the importance of meaningful personal learning, leading with emotional intelligence in the classroom, make intelligent self-direction more understandable and personally relevant.

- **Real-life student and teacher stories** illustrating the value of emotional intelligence and intentional learning in the classroom provide classroom examples of the benefits of person-centered learning over teacher-centered or content-centered learning.

ACKNOWLEDGMENTS

Since the first edition in 2003, there are numerous colleagues we love and respect for their dedication to students, college success, and institutional effectiveness. Likewise there are programs in colleges and organizations that are exemplary applications of our education and transformative model of emotional intelligence.

We want to thank and acknowledge Rick Hammett for joining us in our life's work and contributing original research and ideas to the book. He helped make the book better for students and teachers. Rick Hammett continues to teach EI courses in the doctoral program in educational leadership and graduate programs in adult education and counseling. Spud Reynolds and his creative forces helped make EI come alive for students. Margo Murray, MMHA, The Managers' Mentor, is a friend, and she and her colleagues have used our assessments for many years. Margo has critiqued our work continuously. Ross Ellis has given valuable feedback and direction for our work with education and business. Our professors and mentors in doctoral studies remain with us as we continue our EI work. To John McQuary, Harold Murphy, William E. Truax, Everette Erb, Paul Johnson, and Ruth White, you were our professors, colleagues, friends, and sources of energy and encouragement to extend boundaries of learning and scholarship.

We appreciate the support and acceptance of our work by faculty and students at Texas A&M–Kingsville. Emotional Intelligence has been a topic of interest in academic and support service programs, courses for new students, graduate students in many programs, doctoral students in Educational Leadership and Bilingual Education. Michelle Brown is a valued colleague who directed the doctoral program where 20 EI dissertations were completed since 2002.

We value students and EI colleagues in the United States and globally. Exemplary professionals/organizations using our EI assessments and learning models include

- South Texas College and many colleagues such as Gardner (Spud) Reynolds, Terry Miller, Jorge Botello, Ali Esmaeili, Jose Cruz, Juan Mejia, Shirley Reed, and College Success faculty for their vision in creating a "college-going" culture for students with an emphasis on emotional intelligence.

- Galveston College (Beverly Gammill, Deanna Antosh, and many colleagues and students) for using the ESAP and book in *Achieving the Dream* initiatives and Quality Enhancement Plan.

- San Jacinto College (Rebecca Goosen, Brenda Blue, Myrna Gonzalez, and others) for hosting our 2009 conference; Coastal Bend College (Rito Silva, Jr., Santos Martinez, and many others) for embracing EI for students and staff; College of the Mainland (Cathy Moran, Rebecca Hammett, Stacey Henderson, and others) for supporting our work with students and faculty; Houston Community College (Pam Christian: ACE Fellow, Janis Innis, Zach Hodges, and others);Texas A&M–Commerce (Madeline Justice, Sue Espinoza, and others); Texas A&M–Corpus Christi (Kaye Nelson, Carmen Tejeda-Delgado, Dan Goad, Bob Maroney, Tom Callicott, and others); Tshwane University of Technology (Maryke Botes, Shafeeka Dockrat, and others) for using EI to build college success for students.

- Air University (Patricia Maggard, Hank Dasinger, and others) for infusing ESAP, Personal Excellence Map in self-development and leadership courses.

- Donna M. Rice for extending our research into the importance of EI skills for academic achievement, leadership development, and service learning with the Army's Junior ROTC students and curriculum.

- San Antonio College (Robert Vela, Lisa Black, and many faculty, counselors, and staff) for EI studies and hosting our annual conference and 2010 Institute for Emotional Intelligence.

- Hindustan Petroleum Corporation Limited (Arun Balakrishnan, Ashis Sen, Surya Rao, and many others in HPCL) and FEIL colleagues throughout India for their historic EI initiatives and acceptance of our work.

- Indiana State University (Michael Elkins, David Worley, and others) for their original work integrating EI with communication competence and Servant Leadership.

- Hallmark College (Joe Fisher, Pearl Reyes-Dominguez, and others) for seeing the vision of our life's work with emotional intelligence as a guiding process for leadership programs.

- So many other students and colleagues too numerous to mention throughout Texas, the United States, and the world who inspire students and colleagues who continue to work tirelessly on behalf of students, schools, colleges, and communities.

In 2002, the authors developed a research initiative with emotional intelligence as a forum to disseminate doctoral and external research findings and encourage additional and ongoing research with their education and transformative model of emotional intelligence. In 2004, the authors convened their first annual Institute for Emotional Intelligence to share research with colleagues and highlight "best practice" and exemplary programs using their positive EI assessments, learning systems, and education programs.

The 7th Annual 2010 Institute for Emotional Intelligence was convened in San Antonio, Texas, with the theme *Emotional Intelligence: Developing Teaching and Leadership Excellence*. Now, an international conference with an international journal of emotional intelligence, the Institute has programs relevant to K–12 Education, Higher Education, Business-Organization-Government settings, and Health-Wellness-Counseling.

Contact the authors for information about their assessments, learning systems, and annual Institute for Emotional Intelligence at Emotional Intelligence Learning Systems, Inc. (http://www.eilearningsys.com).

mystudentsuccesslab™

Succeed in college and beyond!
Connect, practice, and personalize with MyStudentSuccessLab.

www.mystudentsuccesslab.com

MyStudentSuccessLab is an online solution designed to help students acquire the skills they need to succeed. They will have access to peer-led video presentations and develop core skills through interactive exercises and projects that provide academic, life, and career skills that will transfer to ANY course.

It can accompany any Student Success text, or be sold as a stand-alone course offering. Often students try to learn material without applying the information. To become a successful learner, they must consistently apply techniques to their daily activities.

MyStudentSuccessLab provides students with opportunities to become successful learners:

Connect:
• Engage with real students through video interviews on key issues.

Practice:
• Three skill-building exercises per topic provide interactive experience and practice.

Personalize:
• Apply what is learned to your life.
• Create a personal project that will be graded and can be posted to your portfolio.
• Journal online and set short- and long-term goals.

JAMES
freshman

MyStudentSuccessLab provides tools and support for students and instructors:

Student Tools/Support – Supplies these tools in addition to the video, exercises, and projects:
  Resources – Use of Plagiarism Guide, Dictionary, Calculators, and a Multimedia index of Interactive case studies and activities.
  Assessments - Includes Career Assessment tool, Learning Styles, and Personality Styles.

Instructor Tools/Support – Saves class prep time and supports implementation while engaging students:
  Sample syllabus – Ensures easy course implementation.
  Instructor's guide – Describes each activity, the skills each addresses, an estimated student time on task for each exercise, and a grading rubric for the final Apply activity.
  Additional Assignments – Suggests extra activities to use with each topic:
  • General activity related to an important objective for each topic.
  • Internet Assignment (e.g. Google "You Tube" video on topic) to find a video on key strategies and write a critique and present it to the class.
  • Resources usage – ie. Read and take online notes on the main points of the Understanding Plagiarism guide.

MyStudentSuccessLab is easy to use and assign. Visit **www.mystudentsuccesslab.com** for additional information. Technical support at http://247pearsoned.custhelp.com.

CUSTOMIZE THIS BOOK WITH

PEARSON LEARNING SOLUTIONS

FOR STUDENT SUCCESS AND CAREER DEVELOPMENT

The Pearson Custom Library Catalog

With Pearson Custom Library, you can create a custom book by selecting content from our course-specific collections. The collections consist of chapters from Pearson titles like this one, and carefully selected, copyright cleared, third-party content, and pedagogy. The finished product is a print-on-demand custom book that students can purchase in the same way they purchase other course materials.

Custom Media

Pearson Learning Solutions works with you to create a customized technology solution specific to your course requirements and needs. We specialize in a number of best practices including custom websites and portals, animation and simulations, and content conversions and customizations.

Custom Publications

We can develop your original material and create a textbook that meets your course goals. Pearson Learning Solutions works with you on your original manuscript to help refine and strengthen it, ensuring that it meets and exceeds market standards. Pearson Learning Solutions will work with you to select already published content and sequence it to follow your course goals.

Online Education

Pearson Learning Solutions offers customizable online course content for your distance learning classes, hybrid courses, or to enhance the learning experience of your traditional in-classroom students. Courses include a fully developed syllabus, media-rich lecture presentations, audio lectures, a wide variety of assessments, discussion board questions, and a strong instructor resource package.

In the end, the finished product reflects your insight into what your students need to succeed, and puts it into practice. Visit us on the web to learn more at www.pearsoncustom.com/studentsuccess 800-777-6872

Darwin Nelson, PhD, is a Consulting Psychologist and Diplomate, American Psychotherapy Association, Patron and Life Member, Forum for Emotional Intelligence Learning (FEIL) in India, and Principal, Emotional Intelligence Learning Systems, Inc. He is cofounder of the Emotional Intelligence Training and Research Institute (EITRI) and has held tenured professorships in Psychology and Education, Texas A&M University–Kingsville. He has taught at every level from secondary to doctoral.

Gary Low, PhD, is Professor Emeritus of Education, Texas A&M University–Kingsville, a Consulting Psychologist, Patron and Life Member, Forum for EI Learning (FEIL) in India, and Principal, Emotional Intelligence Learning Systems, Inc. He is cofounder of the Emotional Intelligence Training and Research Institute (EITRI). He has served as professor, department chair, director of major programs, and dean at Texas A&M–Kingsville. He has developed and taught EI courses for first-generation college students, graduate, and doctoral students.

Friends since first grade and working together since 1977, Darwin Nelson and Gary Low have created, researched, and developed the education, transformative theory and model of emotional intelligence and the Emotional Learning System. Together and individually, they have authored books, articles, and positive assessment instruments used worldwide in education, training, and teaching. Now, spanning four decades, they work collaboratively with educators, organizations, and colleges in designing and implementing EI curricula, programs, and resources to build healthy students, people, organizations, and communities.

Emotional Intelligence and Your Emotional Mind

BELIEFS ABOUT EMOTIONAL INTELLIGENCE AND ACHIEVEMENT

- Emotional intelligence is the single most important influencing variable in personal achievement, career success, leadership, and life satisfaction.

- Emotional intelligence is a learned ability requiring a systematic experience-based approach to learning.

- Schools and colleges do not provide a theory and brain-based practical and systematic model to learn emotional intelligence skills.

- Learning emotional knowledge and skills requires an intentional, active, learner-centered approach involving self-directed coaching, mentoring, and visualization.

- Emotional intelligence consists of specific skills, behaviors, and attitudes that can be learned, applied, and modeled by students to improve personal satisfaction, achievement, and career effectiveness.

Emotional learning that results in increased self-awareness, improved behaviors, and the acquisition of new skills must actively engage the individual in the learning process. Learning by doing and experiencing is the key to learning emotional intelligence skills. This book is designed to help students apply and model the key skills of emotional intelligence in those educational, social, and work settings that demand high levels of achievement and performance. The overall goal of the book is to provide a positive and practical model of human emotional behavior that students can apply to stay mentally, physically, and emotionally healthy; increase achievement and productivity; and improve personal and career performance and satisfaction.

Learning and improving emotional intelligence requires a process that is highly personal, practical, easily understood, and engaging. This text presents 10 basic goals for the student to accomplish:

1. Learn a practical model of emotional intelligence that is essential to success.
2. Identify and explore four competency areas that cover 13 emotional intelligence skills.
3. Develop a meaningful emotional skills profile that emphasizes your strengths.
4. Apply the Emotional Learning System as a personal and career development model.
5. Better understand how the emotional mind works and its positive contributions.
6. Formulate a personal action plan to foster personal and career excellence.
7. Establish and maintain positive, supportive, and healthy relationships.
8. Make positive changes in your understanding and use of emotional skills.
9. Learn, apply, and model stress-management skills to improve your effectiveness.
10. Protect and improve your physical health by learning and applying positive skills.

These goals are focused on helping you improve academic achievement and career performance. Three major learning objectives help you to reduce negative emotional stress; establish, maintain, and enhance healthy intra- and interpersonal relationships; and understand, learn, and apply specific emotional intelligence skills.

TEXT ORGANIZATION

The text is centered on a theory of learning that assumes an individual organizes and learns information by using both thinking (cognitive) and feeling (emotional) systems. It emphasizes a very personal system of learning that actively engages the individual in developing emotional skills. Your primary learning styles are considered, and skill development exercises involve auditory, visual, and kinesthetic (hands-on) activities. Auditory content is presented as text. The text is organized to be experienced and requires active and self-directed involvement.

EMOTIONAL LEARNING SYSTEM

Emotional and experience-based learning is different from traditional academic content learning. The Emotional Learning System is based on this difference. Its five steps are systematic and sequential, yet fluid and interactive—the system is designed to ensure a learner-centered development process built on honest, positive self-assessment. The five steps are as follows:

Step A (Self-Assessment: Explore) requires that you develop an intentional self-assessment habit: inquiring, discovering, and questioning.

Step B (Self-Awareness: Identify) involves the process of identifying your experience as either a thought or a feeling.

Step C (Self-Knowledge: Understand) involves "insight" and an understanding that allows you to make choices about how to behave.

Step D (Self-Development: Learn) involves learning various ways to improve your behavior.

Step E (Self-Improvement: Apply and Model) requires that you apply and model emotionally intelligent behavior to achieve personal, career, and academic goals.

Our belief is that emotional intelligence is best understood and learned when organized and framed around specific emotional skills. Therefore, the text is organized around four competency areas, and each area covers specific emotional intelligence skills.

COMPETENCY AREAS AND RELATED SKILLS

PART I

Interpersonal Skills

■ Assertion is the ability to clearly and honestly communicate personal thoughts and feelings to another person in a comfortable, direct, appropriate, and straightforward manner.

- Aggression is a potential problem area that negatively affects relationships. It involves the anger emotion that must be understood and converted to the Anger Management emotional skill.

- Deference results in ineffective communications that negatively affect relationships. It involves the fear emotion that must be understood and converted to the Anxiety Management emotional skill.

PART II

Leadership Skills

- Social Awareness is the ability to choose the appropriate emotional, social, and physical distance during verbal and nonverbal interactions with others and to affect and influence others in positive ways.

- Empathy is the ability to accurately understand and constructively respond to the expressed feelings, thoughts, behaviors, and needs of others.

- Decision Making is the ability to plan, formulate, initiate, and implement effective problem-solving or conflict-resolution procedures to resolve personal problems and to use a skills approach when making decisions.

- Positive Influence is the ability to positively affect, persuade, and influence others and make a positive difference.

PART III

Self-Management Skills

- Drive Strength is the ability to effectively direct personal energy and motivation to achieve personal, career, and life goals.

- Commitment Ethic is the ability to complete tasks, projects, assignments, and personal responsibilities in a dependable and successful manner, even under difficult circumstances.

- Time Management is the ability to organize tasks into a personally productive time schedule and use time effectively to complete tasks.

- Change Orientation is the degree to which an individual is or is not satisfied and the magnitude of change necessary or desired to develop personal and professional effectiveness. Change Orientation must be understood and converted to the Positive Change emotional skill.

PART IV

Intrapersonal Skills

- Self-Esteem is the ability to view Self as positive, competent, and successful.
- Stress Management is the ability to choose and exercise healthy self-control and self-management in response to stressful events.

Chapters 3 through 6 each address a particular competency area and its relevant skills by applying the Emotional Learning System. Each skill is introduced by way of a definition. The students are then asked to complete a self-assessment to determine their current skill level, which is subsequently plotted on a profile graph. An explanation of the skill follows so that the students can understand the skill and how its use allows them to make choices about their behaviors. Next, the students are invited to learn various techniques that develop the skill. The last step is the application of the various techniques.

PERSONAL CHANGE AND SUCCESS

The most important message of *Emotional Intelligence: Achieving Academic and Career Excellence* is that improving emotional intelligence is a key factor in physical and mental health, academic achievement, personal satisfaction, and career excellence. We have worked with thousands of students and teachers in classes, workshops, and seminars. The obvious seems always to be overlooked or ignored. Almost everyone, at every age and level of development, requires a personal and practical model for experiential or experience-based learning that guides them toward increased emotional self-control and constructive thinking.

Teachers and students have asked for a way to self-renew and keep themselves on a positive and healthy path. Self-renewal and personal excellence are self-defined and self-directed processes that each teacher and student invents and implements in a personally meaningful way. We know and teachers know and students know that emotional intelligence is the key. This text provides a proven lifelong model for learning and developing emotional intelligence skills.

Emotional skill development requires a positive and strength-oriented approach that encourages a person to see changes in the emotional system as a process of continual development and learning. People become stressed and fatigued, and burnout occurs when the demands of work and life exceed internal resources and skills. With this collection of emotional skills, you are in a much better position to take advantage of the opportunities created by stress and personal change.

POSITIVE CONTRIBUTIONS OF YOUR EMOTIONAL MIND

Research is rapidly progressing regarding how the emotional mind works and learns best. Many positive contributions are being discovered and learned by researchers, teachers, and students. When focusing on learning and teaching excellence, it is essential that students and teachers understand that your emotional mind:

- Is the most important influencing factor in high levels of academic achievement and career success;
- Is the key to physical and mental health;
- Enables us to respond to others with empathy and guides our interpersonal interactions with others;
- Makes self-reflection and personal goal setting possible;
- Is the lead system for positive personal change;
- Controls vital survival and stress management functions; and
- Is the lead system and source of happiness, satisfaction, joy, and love.

When you understand, on a personal level, the positive contributions of your emotional mind, you are on the path to becoming an emotionally intelligent student. Build on your uniqueness, and learn each of the emotional intelligence skills as you strive for excellence in your life.

THE EMOTIONALLY INTELLIGENT STUDENT

You are unique in who you are and how you learn. Use the book at your own pace and in a way that complements your learning style. Develop the emotional knowledge and skills that mean the most to you as a person and as a learner. Becoming emotionally intelligent is a lifelong learning process that can keep you happy and healthy. Achieving personal and career excellence is a self-defined and self-directed process. Emotional intelligence skills are a key to your success and your personal well-being.

Unlike traditional academic content, emotional intelligence directly relates to you and how you manage your life and deal with all its important aspects. Thus, developing emotional intelligence skills is a "work in progress." This "work" will yield valuable returns in your life and career as you progress from where you are now to where you want to go throughout your life and your development as a person. Use this book as a guide to fully develop your skills and potential to experience excellence and success in your life and career.

CHAPTER I

Your Emotional Mind

After the first few classes and discussions about emotional intelligence, the learning community students became committed to performing the tasks at hand, and they got into a habit of conducting interactive peer group activities. They used their emotional skills vocabulary in discussion groups regarding their learning experiences. They set realistic goals. Most importantly, they did not "disappear" from the campus; they became comfortable with instructors and peers, and they used the resources on campus. They made meaningful connections.

BEVERLY GAMMILL
English Instructor and EI Coordinator
Galveston College, Galveston, Texas

Preview

E motions are a major part of your personal experience, and few people know, at a practical level, the difference between a thought and a feeling. In fact, many people think that they are opposites and say, "Don't think about it, just do what you feel" or "Follow what your heart says, not your mind." Most people believe that emotions just happen and that there is little they can do about the emotions they experience. Some even go a step further and use emotion as an excuse for their behavior. For example, a college student, explaining to a police officer why he was driving recklessly over the speed limit, said he did it because his girlfriend had made him angry.

The knowledge and skills that you develop to accurately identify and express your emotions are essential to living a long and healthy life. Your physical health is directly related to your ability to regulate and express strong emotions such as anger, fear, and sadness. Although you may not be able to choose your emotions, you can learn to choose how to express them. Regulating the intensity and duration of your strong emotions is a necessary life skill.

THE EMOTIONAL SYSTEM

What Is an Emotion?

An emotion is a feeling state: It is a physiological and physical reaction that is subjectively experienced as strong feelings and physiological changes that prepare the body for immediate action. Emotions are impulses to act. Learning and practicing emotional intelligence (EI) skills allow you to self-direct the impulsive behaviors in a self-valued direction.

Where Do Emotions Come From?

The origin of emotion is the brain. You might say that there are two minds—one that thinks (the thinking mind) and one that feels (the emotional mind). Think of thoughts and emotions as two different mechanisms for knowing and making sense of the world. The two minds are not adversarial or physically separate; rather, they operate interactively to construct your mental life. Passion (the heart) dominates reason (the mind) when feelings are intense.

The amygdala is a structure in the brain that plays an important role in emotion and is where emotional memories are stored. It is the brain's sentry—the first to warn of impending danger. The body's neural pathways for emotions may bypass the neocortex and go directly to the amygdala. This neural shortcut allows the amygdala to receive direct input from the senses and begin a response before the information has reached the neocortex.

What Is the Difference between a Thought and a Feeling?

The ability to distinguish between a thought and a feeling is the foundation of emotionally intelligent behavior. Changing emotional reactivity into self-valued

EXHIBIT 1.1	WHAT ARE THE EMOTIONS THAT WE FEEL?

Circle all the words that identify emotions.

anxiety	pride	anger	pity	contentment
love	excited	tension	satisfied	depressed
hostility	devoted	fear	embarrassed	thrilled
melancholy	friendliness	revenge	laughter	kind
despair	annoyed	sadness	happiness	jealous
worry	confused	apprehensive	dread	delight
envy	gloomy	irritable	concerned	sorrow
outrage	anguish	bliss	panic	shy
frustration	joy	startled	stress	hate
grief	shame	infatuation	boredom	content
nervous	loneliness	trusting	envy	

How many words did you circle?

behavior is a skill called intentionality. The emotional mind is childlike, associative, and often makes mistakes about time. When some features of an event seem similar to an emotionally charged memory, the emotional mind reacts to the present situation as though it was the past. What are the emotions that we all feel and easily recognize? Look at the list of words in Exhibit 1.1 and circle those that identify emotions.

What Are Primary Emotions?

We consider the primary human emotions to be those that everyone in the world recognizes. Look at Exhibit 1.2 and name the emotion expressed by each face.

The four emotions that you labeled are considered primary emotions—those that are universally recognized. Because feelings are important sources of information from the emotional mind, accurately identifying a feeling is calming and frees you from emotional reactivity.

Emotions are experienced in the *present*, and if they are labeled quickly and correctly, you can choose how to behave. Three of the primary emotions—anger, sadness, and fear—can be applied to the diagram shown in Exhibit 1.3.

EXHIBIT 1.2	LABEL THESE EMOTIONS

EXHIBIT 1.3	A TEMPORAL THEORY OF PRIMARY EMOTIONS

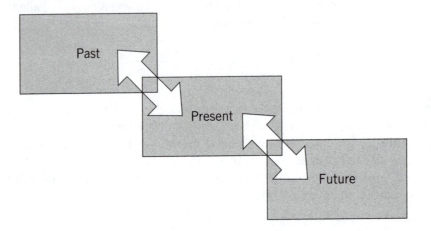

- **Anger** is red hot and signals danger and an attempt to change the *present*—a powerful attempt to stop or start something. Anger tied to the *past* becomes resentment. Anger tied to the *future* becomes envy or jealousy.
- **Sadness** is a blue, empty feeling and signals a physical or psychological loss in the *present*. Sadness tied to the *past* becomes regret, remorse, or guilt. Sadness tied to the *future* becomes pessimism and hopelessness.
- **Fear** is yellow and signals potential danger and the need for caution in the *present*. Traumatic memories from the *past* make you afraid in the present. Fear tied to the *future* becomes worry, anxiety, stress, or panic.

When you have a clear understanding of how the emotional system works and can accurately identify emotions as they are being experienced, you are developing emotional intelligence. The purpose of exploring and developing emotional intelligence is to learn how to achieve self-valued changes in your emotional system.

BREAKING THE EMOTIONAL REACTIVITY HABIT

Most people agree that it is wise to think before you act—thinking is a rational process that improves your ability to behave effectively. At times, you experience strong, almost automatic, emotions that make clear thinking difficult and block constructive or productive behavior. Emotions that are too intense and have a long duration erode your physical and mental health and contribute to self-defeating behavior. The emotional mind is childlike and learns as fast as a developing child. The emotional mind learns through associations and responds to primary emotions such as anger, fear, and sadness. An emotion is a feeling state that is uniquely experienced. Emotions are impulses to act and include both psychological and physical reactions. The tendency to act is a part of the emotional response. It is important to remember that emotions are not neutral. A key aspect of emotional intelligence is to learn how to self-direct and self-monitor your emotional mind.

Emotions are different from thoughts; emotions lead to actions. Without intelligent self-direction and monitoring, emotions naturally lead to a habit of reactivity. Reacting to strong emotions can and often does result in difficult and problematic circumstances. Learning and practicing emotional intelligence skills allows you to self-direct impulsive (quick) behaviors in a self-valued direction. Everyone must have a simple and practical process to understand and deal with strong emotions.

Use the step-by-step ELS process described in Exhibit 1.4, Dealing with Strong Emotions, to understand, identify, label, and express your strong emotions. Practice the process until it becomes a natural, learned response to strong emotions. Remember, strong emotions are an important source of information to be used to improve your behavior—they are neither negative nor positive.

The three emotions that cause people the most difficulty are anger, sadness, and fear. Practicing the step-by-step ELS process will help you change the emotional reactivity habit. Mastering this skill allows you to distinguish between thinking and feeling and to plan and choose self-directed

EXHIBIT 1.4	DEALING WITH STRONG EMOTIONS

Create a personal and truthful model for understanding your emotional Self.

1. Develop emotional self-awareness:
   - Complete the emotional skills assessment process.
   - Clarify your emotional skill strengths and areas to be changed.
   - Self-monitor your emotional responses and patterns.
   - Remind yourself *how* the emotional mind works.

Feelings signal important experiences.

2. Relabel strong emotional responses as an important early warning system that indicates something important is occurring:
   - Feelings (emotions) occur for a reason.
   - Some emotional responses do not have easily accessible cognitive components and occur quickly and automatically.

Emotions are neither negative nor positive; they are human.

3. Nonjudgmental validation of your feelings or emotions:
   - Learn and use positive self-talk.
   - Develop empathic self-assertion (I am having an important feeling, and I can decide how to express it).

Identify the feeling that you are experiencing.

4. Accurately identify and label the emotion:
   - I am happy, sad, angry, or afraid (self-statement).
   - An accurate identification calms the emotional mind (may be due to the involvement of the brain's left lobe, which controls language and logic).

Decide how to express the emotion in a way that is healthy for you and those around you (self-valued change).

5. Personal goal setting or problem solving:
   - Establish clear goals based on value-congruent behaviors.
   - Create options, explore solutions, and choose a behavioral course of action.

(intentional) behaviors instead of reacting to the cues from others or the environment. Research has indicated that self-directed behavior is essential to high levels of achievement, career excellence, and good physical and mental health.

HEALTHY LEARNING ENVIRONMENTS

A healthy learning environment is one in which you learn best—you feel excited about learning and are challenged to think. To create such an environment, you must accept responsibility for your own motivation and learning. Although professors can share their knowledge and information with you, help you identify important concepts, and introduce you to new ways of thinking and solving problems, they cannot teach you anything that you are not willing to learn. Students who wait to be motivated by their professors often wait a very long time. Those students describe themselves as "bored" or "unmotivated"—they've slipped into a reactive mode while waiting for some external force to motivate or excite them.

When you have passion (feeling for and interest in) about an idea or subject, learning is rapid, effortless, and personally satisfying. This is the work of the emotional mind—it is always easier to learn about things that you like and enjoy. Those subjects or areas that you have little interest in are more difficult to learn and require a different learning strategy. Become aware of how you learn best by identifying your unique learning style, then seek out learning resources on campus that can help you master the difficult or uninteresting assignments. You might organize a group of friends supportive of academic excellence, join organizations that provide learning resources and stress academic success, find a mentor who is interested in your goals, or seek help from professors who model scholarship and value lifelong learning.

Drive and motivation are internal processes that you must learn to access and direct to achieve meaningful goals. Although a master teacher can help create a learning environment that engages and challenges you, it is ultimately up to you to develop your mind to its fullest potential.

STRESS, BURNOUT, AND BOREDOM

Stress is an unavoidable part of living and can be either positive or negative. Finishing high school and making the transition to college is a major source of stress. For some students, the transition's stress and excitement are somewhat overwhelming—they forget to go to class and to study. They excel at the university's covert curriculum, but are graded on the cognitive. They have a great time—but only for a short period. A student's ability to manage stress is a key emotional intelligence skill because negative stress (distress) and intense emotions experienced over a long period of time are physically harmful. Moderate anxiety (fear) about an upcoming quiz may motivate you to study the material instead of spending time with a friend. Some anxiety serves a beneficial purpose when it warns of impending danger—too much anxiety, however, can hinder your performance and lower your achievement. Emotionally reactive students experience burnout and boredom. They lack the energy to focus on challenging assignments that require long periods of concentrated effort.

When your parents and friends waved good-bye as you left for college, many of them said, "Take good care of yourself." What they meant was "have a good time and learn to manage the stress you will experience from the change." The best buffer against negative stress is a positive, supportive relationship. Everyone is occasionally overwhelmed by stress when demands are greater than available internal resources. We sometimes lack the emotional, physical, or financial resources necessary to manage and solve an immediate crisis. Involve yourself in friendships. Establish a relationship with a mentor who values you as a person and who will encourage and support you during times of personal crises.

COLLEGE SUCCESS FACTORS

The transitions from high school to college and from college to career can be exciting times for you. These are the transitions that are essential to your personal, academic, and career success. How you manage these changes is directly related to how you manage yourself in response to the demands and pressures of academic work and career challenges.

A well-kept secret for over 200 years is that colleges and universities have *two* important curricula. One curriculum is cognitive and focuses on academic content areas, grade point averages, semester hours, and academic honor societies. It is this curriculum that most students describe when asked what constitutes "higher education"—the mastery of course content and the accumulation of semester hours. Each discipline has its own content that is divided into courses that are completed one at a time. When enough courses are finished, a degree is awarded. The other curriculum is covert (less visible) and is not as rational, focused, or organized—we call it the emotional or

EXHIBIT 1.5	THE EMOTIONAL CURRICULUM ATTITUDES AND BEHAVIORS

- Achieve a balance between the cognitive and the emotional mind.
- Develop active listening skills.
- Identify and use your primary learning style.
- Use campus resources to improve your reading speed and comprehension.
- Develop time-management and self-management skills.
- Set personal goals (Drive Strength).
- Be organized, punctual, and dependable (Commitment Ethic and Time Management).
- Be assertive with yourself, friends, and professors (Assertion).
- Effectively manage and express strong emotions (Stress Management).
- Appreciate and value difference (Empathy and Positive Influence).
- Focus on your strengths (Self-Esteem).
- Establish and maintain healthy relationships (Social Awareness and Decision Making).
- Recognize and express emotions effectively (Anger and Anxiety Management).
- Be flexible (Positive Change).

covert curriculum. It is, however, just as important to your academic and career success as the cognitive curriculum.

The covert curriculum is not primarily based on what you are supposed to do; rather, it is based on relationships, social activities, fun, adventure, recreation, collegiate sports and organizations, and what you want to do at any particular time. The emotional curriculum consists of skill-related attitudes and behaviors that occur both inside and outside the classroom (see Exhibit 1.5).

These attitudes and behaviors comprise a major part of your experience as a student. When you know how your emotional mind works and how to apply emotional intelligence skills, you are on your way to personal, academic, and career success.

Briefly scan Exhibit 1.6, College Success Factors. How many are related to the covert curriculum, requiring emotionally intelligent decisions and behaviors? Emotional intelligence behaviors are transferable lifelong skills—employers look for them during interviews, and they are necessary to develop healthy interpersonal relationships.

EXHIBIT 1.6	COLLEGE SUCCESS FACTORS

- Establish a positive, supportive relationship with a person (mentor) who is interested in you and your success.
- Know how to locate and access campus resources.
- Establish meaningful personal goals related to successful college completion.
- Create a daily schedule and track your progress.
- Commit to your primary "career" by being a good student.
- Identify, maximize, and expand your personal learning style.
- Form a study or support group.
- Initiate contact with professors, teaching assistants, and high-achieving students.
- Develop critical-thinking skills.
- Choose classes with professors who support your learning style.
- Know how and where to get information.
- Improve your writing and speaking skills.
- Learn the career life-planning process and visit the career center.
- Build friendships with peers who are committed to academic and career success.
- Learn, practice, and strengthen assertive communication skills.
- Get involved in a campus organization that supports your interests.
- Improve your physical wellness skills.
- Become computer literate and build your word-processing skills.
- Attend all classes.
- Increase your personal expectations with each success.

HIGH ACHIEVEMENT AND SELF-DIRECTED LEARNING

Students who reach high levels of academic and career achievement are self-directed learners who master both the cognitive and emotional curricula. Sternberg (1995) characterized successful intelligent people as those who:

- Are initiators who motivate themselves
- Learn to control their impulses and delay gratification
- Know how to persevere and seek to surmount personal difficulties

- Translate thought into action and do not procrastinate
- Complete tasks and follow through
- Are not afraid to risk failure, accept responsibility, and reject self-pity
- Are independent and focus on personally meaningful goals
- Balance their thinking (cognitive with emotional)
- Possess self-confidence and positive self-efficacy

Our research, conducted over the past 30 years, has supported Sternberg's description—a description that reflects the essential characteristics or skills of the emotionally intelligent student. Learning to apply and model these skills greatly enhances your chance for success.

Exhibit 1.7, An Emotionally Intelligent Student's Characteristics, sets forth the attitudes and behaviors necessary for academic and, ultimately, career success. Remember, emotionally intelligent students are proactive—not reactive.

Emotionally intelligent behavior involves understanding your immediate experience and learning to think constructively about your behavior choices; it requires exercising good judgment and acting wisely (intelligent self-direction). The Emotional Learning System (discussed in Chapter 2) provides a model for learning emotional skills and applying them in active, integrative, and personally meaningful ways.

EXHIBIT 1.7	AN EMOTIONALLY INTELLIGENT STUDENT'S CHARACTERISTICS

Emotionally Reactive Student	Emotionally Intelligent Student
Overwhelmed too often	Resilient
Reactive to stress	Proactive, planned responses to stress
Emotionally driven behavior	Intentional reflective behavior
Self-doubting	Self-confident
Deficit and weakness focused	Strength focused
Resistant to change	Flexible; open to change
Aggressive, nonassertive communicator	Assertive communicator
Performance decreases under stress	Performance improves under stress
Pessimistic, sarcastic, negative focus	Optimistic, positive, hopeful focus
Relies on reactive habits	Relies on positive habits
Continually makes the same mistakes	Learns from experience

TWELVE IMPORTANT LESSONS

We have researched and studied the effect and impact of personal and emotional skills on human performance and blended that information with our own professional experience as college educators and consultants to business and industry—the result was the development of 12 lessons that have major implications for the way we study, work, and live on an everyday basis. Emotional learning and emotional intelligence make significant contributions to high achievement, career excellence, personal leadership, and quality performance. You can benefit from learning how to develop your emotional intelligence, not out of necessity, but out of a personal commitment to improve success, your personal well-being, and your academic and career performance.

To gain the most from this text, try to internalize and learn from each of the 12 lessons and corresponding hallmarks of our transformational approach to emotional intelligence. Make a personal decision to fully develop your emotional intelligence. This intentional and active decision is the key.

Lesson

Lesson 1. Some people believe that people cannot substantively change.

Lesson 2. Life's emotional aspect is the most important. Although this is true for everyone, the emotional dimension is missing from or neglected by most educational programs.

Lesson 3. High levels of achievement, success, and happiness are self-defined and self-directed.

Lesson 4. Honest self-assessment is necessary for positive and intentional personal change. Even so, most assessments and evaluations do not acknowledge this and do not take a positive, formative, and developmental approach.

Educational Corollaries: Hallmarks of the Transformative Model of EI

Hallmark 1. Reflective and constructive thinking processes can be effectively taught and learned. Reflective and constructive thinking engenders emotionally intelligent and wise behavior.

Hallmark 2. Approaching affective education as an integrated set of learned abilities based on specific emotional skills provides a straightforward approach for learning and teaching emotional intelligence.

Hallmark 3. Including and integrating the emotional system in constructive, intentional ways enhances academic and life success.

Hallmark 4. Positive assessment models, such as those provided in this text, are key.

Lesson 5. Students learn best and work best in environments that are physically and emotionally safe. High levels of performance and productivity are easier to achieve and sustain when trust, respect, communication, commitment, and personal leadership are evident in safe environments.

Hallmark 5. Transformative approaches emphasize trust, support, and affirmation to engender personal meaning and instill intelligent self-direction.

Lesson 6. Emotional intelligence is the most important factor in achieving excellence. Even so, most people have not been provided systematic opportunities to learn EI competencies and skills.

Hallmark 6. Education models must incorporate a systematic or step-by-step process for learning and teaching EI.

Lesson 7. The effects of negative and unchecked emotional stress and ineffective or poor relationships are financially costly. The human costs that result from poor health, destructive relationships, and a loss of hope for a better life cause even more long-term damage.

Hallmark 7. Although a degree of independence is important for success in life, ultimately interdependence is more important than independence. Healthy, effective relationships are essential for superior performance and outstanding personal and organizational leadership.

Lesson 8. A personal and emotional accountability system is essential for high achievement.

Hallmark 8. The Emotional Learning System and positive assessment processes provide a model for building personal and emotional accountability around the emotional intelligence competencies and associated emotional skills.

Lesson 9. People develop and change themselves. People have within themselves all they need to live productive, responsible, and satisfying lives, although they may require some help to know what to learn and how to make positive changes.

Hallmark 9. Our minds are shaped by how we process and relate with the important events and feelings in our lives. The Emotional Learning System provides a systematic way to constructively process important life events and feelings.

Lesson 10. The four critical areas of human performance are Interpersonal, Personal Leadership, Self-Management, and Intrapersonal. These performance areas represent the essential competencies or component areas of emotional intelligence.

Hallmark 10. To be transformational, EI assessments must include these four areas of human performance.

Lesson 11. Personal meaning is more powerful than external data. The individual determines personal meaning. Emotional growth and health are exciting, enjoyable, and rewarding, but must have a foundation of personal meaning.

Hallmark 11. Intelligent self-direction, which is a by-product of studying and learning about emotional intelligence, results from emotional reflection and learning, higher-order thinking, (thinking about how we think and feel), and healthy functioning.

The last lesson, **Lesson 12**, is simply that life transitions and changes are often challenging and sometimes difficult. The educational corollary or hallmark of transformational EI is that developing a healthy emotional mind must be intentional, skill based, and it requires protection, permission, and personal empowerment. *EI Man* provides a wonderful and interesting example of this lesson in Exhibit 1.8, The Hermit Crab Story. In many ways, the process of successfully developing and exercising your emotional intelligence in life closely parallels the healthy growth and success of the Hermit Crab.

EXHIBIT 1.8	LESSONS FROM THE HERMIT CRAB

How Do I Grow?

From a story by Dr. Darwin Nelson Adapted by Gardner Reynolds

Once upon a time, there was a very young Hermit Crab. He was so young he really didn't understand how fragile he was. He never knew his mother or father. They were carried off and eaten by seagulls right after he was born. He soon discovered that, although the front of his body, his claws and his head were covered by a hard shell, his whole back end was like mush; really, really soft. He knew he needed to get a house to live in to protect himself. And he better do it pretty quickly, for he heard the dreaded, dangerous seagulls all the time.

One day when he was very carefully exploring the beach, he found an old shell. He poked his claws into it and looked around. "Wow," he thought, "It's empty. I could live in here!" and he quickly slipped his rear end in the shell.

He lived very comfortably in the shell for quite a while. But one day he woke up with a bad backache. He pulled himself out of the shell a little way and the pain stopped. He tried to push himself back in and the pain came back. He soon realized he had outgrown his shell-house and he needed a bigger one. So he dragged his old shell around very carefully all over the beach until he found another shell. It was bigger, so said good-bye and moved in to his new house.

After a while, the back pain happened again, so he went looking for even bigger shell. Again, he knew he was vulnerable and had to be very careful. But this time, he learned a new lesson: He was going to keep growing and he would need even bigger shells, so he scoured the beach looking for even bigger shells. He found several more and dragged them all to the same place so he had them when he needed them. This was one smart Hermit Crab!

In many ways, people are like Hermit Crabs. Not so much on the outside, our bodies get bigger and we need bigger clothes, sure, but where we really grow, and sometimes are vulnerable and need protection, is on the inside: Our minds and feelings need to grow. Our souls need to expand and adapt to include new situations as we journey through life.

We go from being babies to children in a family, then we go to school, to church to be married and then out into the world to seek our fortunes.

Many times along the path in life, we will meet new people, go to new schools, get new jobs, become a parent and raise a family, go into the hospital, or feel the pain of a loss of a loved one. All kinds of new things happen to us, some are fun and some are not so fun, but every time something big and important and new happens to us, we need to grow inside to meet the challenge.

When something new happens to you, how do you deal with it? Well, you can be like an ostrich; hide your head in the sand and go into denial and pretend nothing is happening. Or you can get like a rattlesnake; coil up and get all hostile, ready to strike out at anybody that comes near you. Or be like a scorpion in a fire and sting yourself to death. Probably, not too smart.

On the more positive side, you could be like a baby chicken. When she gets too big for her shell, she pokes her beak through it and out she comes: Here I am world, ready or not.

Or better yet, why not be like a Hermit Crab? Push the envelope and find a bigger house for yourself. Sure, you need to be careful when you're looking for your new place, but there's nothing wrong with the "Spirit of Adventure." It can be very cool to expand your mind & spirit and grow. Think of all the new things you will learn. Think of how you will feel about yourself about being a "risk-taker" who found a new way that worked.

(Continued)

The Good Lord didn't put us here to be stuck inside an old shell. Your ego, what you mean when you say "I am," needs to change and grow in a positive way. Being stuck in an overgrown ego that thinks it's better than everybody else is a major drag. But having an "I am" that blends and flows with all the other "I am's" makes life enjoyable for you and everybody around you.

It's very uncool to be stuck in a rut. It hurts to be all cramped up in a hard shell. Life is all about taking chances, expanding your mind and feelings, adapting to changes and learning new things. So maybe take a lesson from our little buddy, the Hermit Crab.

LINK

Very few people develop the knowledge and skills to integrate thinking and feeling into effective behaviors. Emotions are often viewed as automatic and beyond conscious control. You may not be able to choose when you feel, but you can learn to control how you experience and express your emotions. The next chapter outlines the important steps in becoming an emotionally intelligent student. A very practical model for understanding your emotional mind is presented. Understanding the emotional mind leads to constructive thinking, and constructive thinking leads to more effective (successful) behavior. As you learn more about how the emotional mind works, you will begin to view personal behavior as what you do more than how you are.

CHAPTER 2

Developing an Emotionally Healthy Mind

This book may be meant to help students be more successful, but I have found that it will benefit the reader in every aspect of life, not just school. Even if you think you have it all together, I think you might find something in this book that will help you be even better.

STUDENT
*Galveston College,
Galveston, Texas*

Preview

T he twenty-first century's growing global economy, with its inherent rapid changes, provides a compelling case for the need to develop an emotionally intelligent population. People learn and work best in environments that are physically and psychologically safe. Developing leadership qualities, building effective teams, and reaching high levels of quality production involve several emotional elements—trust, communication, respect, motivation, and personal commitment. Emotional intelligence (EI) skills are vital to human performance and healthy, productive organizations. Physical health and personal well-being are directly related to a person's ability to understand the emotional mind and to use constructive thinking to guide behavior.

The focus of this chapter is on the theory, specific skills, and the behaviors necessary for academic and career excellence, emotional self-control, and healthy interpersonal relationships based on a transformative approach to EI. We encourage you to read Appendix A for additional information, as well as other literature to learn more about these other important perspectives and contributions to the field.

Ours is an education and skill-based approach. It is a conception of Emotional Intelligence in which excellence is viewed as an intentional commitment to high levels of achievement, work quality, and personal well-being—it is self-defined, self-directed, and based on specific EI skills.

Two tools are explained in Chapter 2 that will be used throughout the text. The Emotional Learning System (ELS) and the Emotional Skills Assessment Process (ESAP) are tools developed by the authors to learn and teach EI in a way that respects the hallmarks of the education model (see Chapter 1, Lessons and Hallmarks) of emotional intelligence. Helpful learning strategies are also discussed as you strive toward achieving academic and career excellence.

THE EMOTIONAL LEARNING SYSTEM

Knowing and applying the ELS gives you an important guide to understanding your immediate experience. By understanding and using the information received from both your cognitive and experiential systems, you can learn to choose behavior based on constructive and critical thinking. This is called intentional behavior. With practice, intentional behaviors become habitual and automatic. Intentional behavior is reflective behavior. Conversely, reactive behavior is impulse driven, almost automatic, and is occasionally done without thought or awareness. Impulsive behavior is self-defeating in academic, corporate, and personal relationships. People who are perpetually reactive and self-defeating may lack a personal theory for understanding relationships in a constructive and emotionally healthful way. The education model of emotional intelligence provides such a framework.

We agree with Seymour Epstein's (1998) view of constructive thinking as a key to emotional intelligence. A major premise of his theory is that humans have two minds or systems that receive and process experiences. The emotional mind is unconscious, works and reacts very quickly, and relies primarily on experience for knowing. The cognitive mind works more slowly, is more systematic, and works to protect our emotional system. To act wisely and exercise good judgment, you must learn to balance both minds. An essential skill to developing emotionally intelligent behavior is the ability to assess your immediate experience—your current thoughts, feelings, and behaviors.

EXHIBIT 2.1	THE EMOTIONAL LEARNING SYSTEM

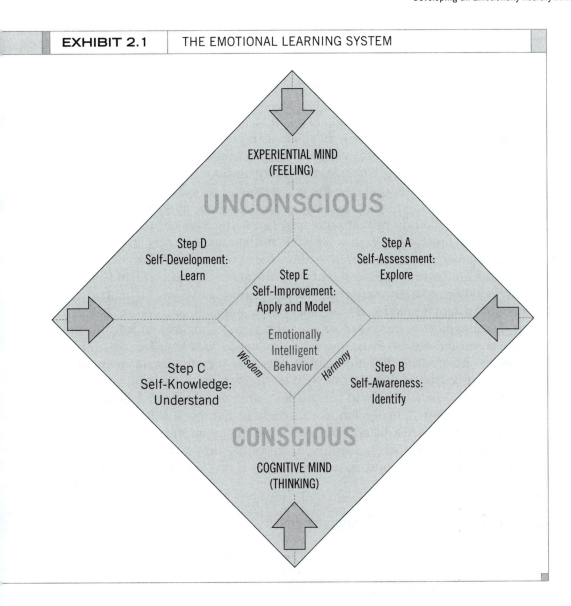

Exhibit 2.1 illustrates the ELS and how the various components are connected and work together. The upper portion of the diagram represents your experiential or unconscious mind; the lower portion represents your cognitive or conscious mind. The ELS uses five steps to process an experience. There is a flow between the experiential and cognitive minds as each step is accomplished. Without an intentional approach to developing ourselves in a healthy way, the tendency is to be reactive when we have strong feelings. In reactive states, the five steps of emotional learning still take place, but the resulting behaviors can be quite self-defeating and unintended.

Many people may be under the false impression that when they experience an emotionally charged event, they just have an automatic reaction and almost involuntary behavior. Despite this popular belief, reactions to emotionally charged events are not automatic. Your emotional reactions to important events in your life are based on how your emotional mind has developed (remember the amygdala?) and the degree to which your cognitive mind is able to interpret those events constructively. However, the pattern of your reactions will tend to be based on any unconscious interpretations of the events taking place. Unconscious interpretations, in turn, are influenced heavily by the experiential system and emotional memories.

Unconscious interpretations of our experiences are most easily conceptualized as thought processes that occur just below the level of full consciousness. This is why Epstein (1998) has referred to them as occurring in the "preconscious." Many people are not even aware of their preconscious thoughts, yet these thoughts are natural, are persistent, and influence our feelings and behavior every waking moment. We all can become more aware of our preconscious thoughts through practice. By becoming more aware of your feeling states, you can become more conscious of your preconscious thoughts and learn to think more constructively. By increasing your awareness about your feelings and practicing to enhance specific emotional skills, you will gradually and naturally become more self-directed and effective in the pursuit of your self-valued goals.

To facilitate self-valued and personally meaningful change, it is helpful to understand the Basic Change Process outlined in Exhibit 2.2. Positive personal change is achieved first by acknowledging the importance of your thoughts, beliefs, and values and then by learning to critically examine your behavior within that context. Becoming a constructive thinker is best achieved by intentionally

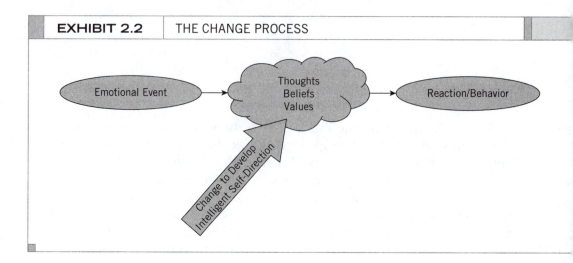

EXHIBIT 2.2 THE CHANGE PROCESS

applying and routinely practicing the ELS in a way that brings emotional learning from the preconsciousness, unintended realm into the realm of conscious thought. The ELS is expanded in Exhibit 2.3 to illustrate this more intentional application. When confronted with strong feelings, use the five steps of the ELS in a systematic process to become less reactive and to better understand, identify, label, and constructively express your strong emotions. Practice the ELS process with the goal of making the reflective process feel as natural as the urge to react. Remember, a strong emotion is an important source of information that you can use to improve your effectiveness and happiness. Emotion is neither negative nor positive, and it only becomes a problem when experienced intensely for too long or when it leads to self-destructive behavior.

Step A (Self-Assessment: Explore) requires that you develop an intentional self-assessment habit: inquiring, discovering, and questioning (e.g., What thoughts am I having right now? What am I feeling? How do I want to respond to this situation?). Because self-assessment is the active process of exploring your experience as it occurs, you must pause before you act. Even when strong emotions (e.g., anger, fear, or sadness) dominate your immediate experience, the self-assessment process enables you to pause so that you can follow the path of reflection, not reaction.

Step B (Self-Awareness: Identify) involves the process of identifying your experience as either a thought or a feeling. Accurate self-awareness is the ability to correctly identify and label the emotion being experienced. Once the emotion is identified, the constructive-thinking process can begin.

Step C (Self-Knowledge: Understand) involves "insight" and an understanding that allows you to make choices about how to behave. Wise actions are the immediate result of conscious reflection and constructive thinking. Occasionally, Step C is a logical and sequential process. At other times, a quick "insight" pops into your awareness, and you can see new, more creative, and better problem-solving options.

Step D (Self-Development: Learn) involves learning various ways to improve your behavior. Positive self-development is a learning process—seldom is our behavior correct on the first attempt. Improved behavior requires choosing and engaging in personal behavior that pleases you and increases your self-esteem and self-appreciation. New and improved behaviors require practice to become intentional habits.

Step E (Self-Improvement: Apply and Model) requires that you apply and model emotionally intelligent behavior to achieve personal, career, and academic goals. The ability to apply and model emotionally intelligent behavior is not an "arrival" state; rather, it is a process of using the preceding four steps to achieve your best as a person.

Wisdom and *harmony* are words used to describe the balance you achieve when you use both the cognitive and experiential minds to guide

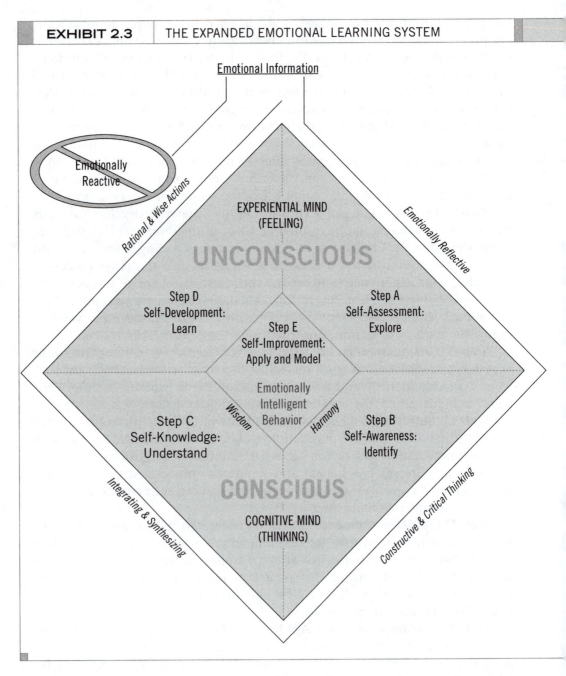

EXHIBIT 2.3   THE EXPANDED EMOTIONAL LEARNING SYSTEM

Emotional Information

Emotionally Reactive

Rational & Wise Actions

Emotionally Reflective

EXPERIENTIAL MIND
(FEELING)

UNCONSCIOUS

Step D
Self-Development:
Learn

Step A
Self-Assessment:
Explore

Step E
Self-Improvement:
Apply and Model

Emotionally
Intelligent
Behavior

Wisdom

Harmony

Step C
Self-Knowledge:
Understand

Step B
Self-Awareness:
Identify

CONSCIOUS

Integrating & Synthesizing

Constructive & Critical Thinking

COGNITIVE MIND
(THINKING)

your behavior choices. Emotions signal a significant experience and generate
an impulse to act. Behavior is more effective when it is guided by reflective
and constructive thought. A wise person exhibits good judgment in the present, based on experience. People behave wisely when they understand and
use both minds in harmony.

APPLYING THE EMOTIONAL LEARNING SYSTEM

The ELS is a step-by-step process that helps your thinking become more emotionally reflective and constructive. As you become more reflective and constructive, you will be more aware of your choice of behavior. The system is a process that helps you balance your feelings and thoughts by choosing intentional behaviors that are called emotional intelligence skills.

For you to model emotionally intelligent behavior on a daily basis, you must access and complete this process of learning each time that you want to improve or change a thought, feeling, or behavior. Positive self-development and personal change are constant lifelong processes.

Exhibit 2.4 outlines the steps of the learning system and how each step is completed for each emotional intelligence skill. Developing intentional behavior habits is achieved by consistently practicing and working through the system.

EXHIBIT 2.4	APPLYING THE EMOTIONAL LEARNING SYSTEM

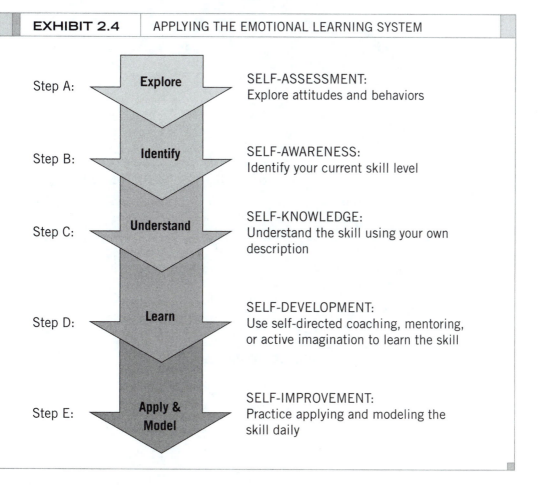

Step A: **Explore**
SELF-ASSESSMENT:
Explore attitudes and behaviors

Step B: **Identify**
SELF-AWARENESS:
Identify your current skill level

Step C: **Understand**
SELF-KNOWLEDGE:
Understand the skill using your own description

Step D: **Learn**
SELF-DEVELOPMENT:
Use self-directed coaching, mentoring, or active imagination to learn the skill

Step E: **Apply & Model**
SELF-IMPROVEMENT:
Practice applying and modeling the skill daily

LEARNING STYLES

Before you can begin to learn and develop the 13 emotional intelligence skills, it may be helpful to identify your preferred way of learning. Exhibit 2.5 applies four particular learning styles to the ELS process. Look at Exhibit 2.5 and think about the representational systems or learning processes that you prefer or favor when learning from your immediate experience.

EXHIBIT 2.5	LEARNING STYLES AND THE EMOTIONAL LEARNING SYSTEM

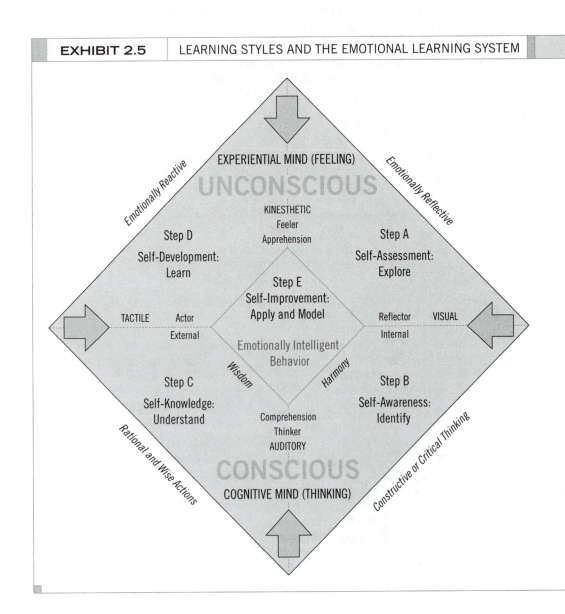

Is your personal learning style auditory, visual, tactile, or kinesthetic? No one is a pure "type," so it is helpful to identify your preferred learning approach. Decide whether you favor an auditory approach (learning from what you hear), a visual approach (learning from what you see), or a kinesthetic or tactile approach (learning from what you feel—hands-on activities).

Visual learners benefit from pictures, visual imagery, mind mapping, rehearsal techniques, and video approaches to learning. "I need to see how to do that" is an example of visual learning. Kinesthetic and tactile learners benefit from mentors and hands-on strategies. Facilitated mentoring relationships, interactive learning via the Internet, and self-formed study and support groups may be the key to this learning approach. "I need to actually do the activity to learn it" is an example of kinesthetic and tactile learning.

Auditory

Auditory learners benefit from *self-directed coaching*. Positive self-talk, audio recordings, and teaching strategies emphasizing listening may be the key to auditory learning. "A good lecture is all I need to hear" is what an auditory learner might say. Following is a checklist of the self-directed coaching features and learning ideas (with space to add your own).

___ Be information and logic oriented	___ Develop strategic game plan
___ Gather resources	___ Set high goals
___ Develop a plan	___ Self-direct your efforts to a goal
___ Use positive self-talk	___ Rehearse and practice
___ Remind yourself to listen	___ Intentionally have a positive plan
___ Know your strengths	___ Plan ahead to act, not react
___ Ask for help	___ Remind yourself to relax

Visual

Visual learners can benefit from using the *active imagination strategy*. This strategy uses positive imagery and mind mapping to improve academic and career success. Following is a checklist of some ideas for using the active imagination strategy. Develop other ideas and add them to the list.

____ Use positive imagery	____ Create successful goal images
____ Rehearse through imagery	____ Relax and focus
____ Increase practice with pictures	____ Mentally draw your plan with word pictures
____ Use mind maps	
____ Visually image confidence	____ Learn from successful models
____ Mentally practice/rehearse	____ Map out your strategy using colors and symbols
____ Create visual associations	
____ Watch for success behaviors	____ Use imagery to increase memory

____ _____   ____ _____

____ _____   ____ _____

____ _____   ____ _____

____ _____   ____ _____

Kinesthetic and Tactile

Kinesthetic and tactile learners benefit from using the *emotional mentoring strategy*. This learning style uses feelings, hands-on activities, and successful models to improve performance. Following is a checklist of some ideas for using the emotional mentoring strategy. Work with your mentor to develop other ideas and add them to the list.

____ Observe successful models	____ Use models similar to your style
____ Ask a mentor for feedback	____ Rehearse, observe performance
____ Find and use a mentor	____ Build confidence by practicing
____ Practice over and over	____ Focus on skills and feelings
____ Teach, show someone	____ Ask a mentor to show you how to do something
____ Practice relaxation	
____ Use verbal and nonverbal behaviors	____ Use feelings as a signal to practice constructive and critical thinking
____ Use intuition to complement critical thinking	

_____   _____   _____   _____
_____   _____   _____   _____
_____   _____   _____   _____
_____   _____   _____   _____
_____   _____   _____   _____
_____   _____   _____   _____

In our experience, kinesthetic learners may greatly improve their academic achievement by using visual and auditory learning strategies. Without a systematic approach to learning using auditory and visual cues, kinesthetic learners actively and quickly move from feelings to action. In many cases, this leads to reactive rather than reflective behavior. Constructive, reflective thinking is a skill dimension that kinesthetic learners must develop.

Each learning style is a good way to learn from academic and life experiences. Each approach provides ideas to incorporate for study and practice. An emotionally intelligent student develops a variety of learning approaches to take advantage of each learning style. Be aware of the impact and importance of sound, pictures, and feelings in understanding your experience and in how you learn best.

LEARNING STRATEGIES

To learn and improve your emotional intelligence, you must remember that a feeling is a signal to think about how you want to behave. When you actively and intentionally practice the learned ability of emotional intelligence, you are integrating the cognitive (thinking) mind and emotional (feeling) mind. Thoughts and emotions are two different ways of knowing and making sense of our world. As you learn emotional intelligence, you discover that the two systems are not adversarial or physically separate but operate interactively and in harmony to construct our mental outlook. Passion (the heart) dominates reason (the mind) when feelings are intense.

Three primary strategies can be used to improve your emotional skills: self-directed coaching, emotional mentoring, and active imagination. These new learning processes enable the emotional mind to learn quickly and work effectively with the cognitive mind to achieve new levels of excellence in your life. Each of these strategies uses active, intentional, and intelligent self-direction and monitoring to learn, improve, and apply emotional intelligence on a daily and consistent basis. The strategies are based on your unique learning style, and because your learning style may comprise several different styles, it may be necessary to use more than one. Exhibit 2.6 demonstrates the importance

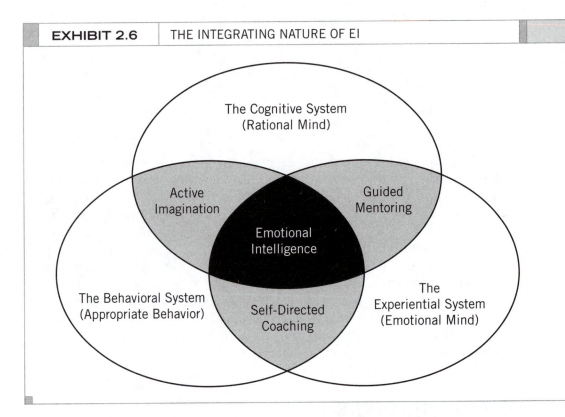

EXHIBIT 2.6 | THE INTEGRATING NATURE OF EI

of the three primary learning strategies for integrating the emotional, cognitive, and behavioral systems to shape intelligent self-direction.

Self-Directed Coaching

Self-directed coaching is an integrated, confluent learning process guided by an auditory approach to emotional learning that requires you to develop a strategic game plan to learn the principles and skills of emotional intelligence. This strategy involves setting high goals, developing a plan, and directing your efforts with intentional, consistent, and skilled attitudes and behaviors. Because self-directed coaching is logic and information oriented, it might be a useful strategy for those with auditory or logical–mathematical learning styles. Internet resources and interactive learning programs are also useful.

Emotional Mentoring

Emotional mentoring is an integrated, confluent learning process guided by a kinesthetic approach to emotional learning. Emotional skills can be learned through the observation and modeling that occurs in a mentoring relationship.

People with a kinesthetic learning style benefit from this method. Emotional mentors might use the targeted skills from the ESAP as a teaching model.

Active Imagination

Active imagination involves the use of positive imagery for relaxation, action goal setting, and stress management. Students with a visual learning style might find this strategy helpful. The brain is constantly manufacturing thoughts and pictures—whether you are aware of them or not—and most of these randomly produced thoughts and images are either neutral or negative. If you want pleasant experiences and feelings, you must intentionally create them. Use the steps shown in Exhibit 2.7, Active Imagination, to create good feelings and images.

EXHIBIT 2.7	ACTIVE IMAGINATION	
STEP	**CLUE(S)**	**NOTES**
1. Think of a past event that was very pleasant.	What was happening? What were you doing? Sort through your memory and focus on a pleasant scene.	
2. Close your eyes and picture the scene.	Ensure that you are seeing what you saw when the pleasant event occured.	
3. Make the scene vivid and sensory loaded.	What colors do you see? What sounds do you hear? What things do you feel, taste, or smell?	
4. As you look at and experience the scene, brighten the image; then, dim the image.	Changing the brightness of the image can change your feelings.	I feel _____ when I brighten the image and _____ when I dim it.
5. Use your pleasant image daily.	Use the image to relax. Practice controlling the experience.	

Because the emotional mind learns more effectively when you use intelligent self-direction and self-monitoring, you should learn and use one or more of the strategies to improve your emotional intelligence.

NECESSARY CONDITIONS FOR LEARNING

To improve and maximize emotional learning, most people have personal needs that must be addressed. They also have to know that this emotional skill development will somehow help them in their efforts to achieve success and excellence in their lives. Emotional learning requires a personal commitment to develop and practice emotional skills. When certain conditions are met, emotional learning is easier, faster, and better. These necessary conditions encompass a set of beliefs and features that create an environment conducive to learning:

- Acknowledge each person as competent with dignity, worth, and potential.
- Commit to responsible growth and effective behaviors.
- Emphasize the skills and competencies of emotional intelligence.
- Empower each person to make positive changes and move forward in life.
- Respect the capacity of each person to achieve excellence.
- Identify and organize specific skill sets that can be easily learned and applied.
- Base learning and development on honest self-assessment and your internal frame of reference.
- Demystify emotional behavior by learning new ways to think, act, and feel.

CHANGING YOUR EMOTIONAL MIND

Improving emotional intelligence is an internal, self-directed process. Mental harmony (happiness, contentment, and satisfaction) occurs when your thoughts and feelings are in tune. Thoughts influence feelings, and feelings influence thinking. How you think, feel, and choose behaviors is a reflection of your unique picture of yourself and your interpretation and interaction with your immediate environment. The internal frame of reference, how things appear to you, is an important starting point for developing self-awareness.

Emotional intelligence is a confluence of developed skills and abilities to: (1) accurately know yourself, feel valuable, and behave responsibly as a person of worth and dignity; (2) establish and maintain a variety of effective, strong, and healthy relationships; (3) get along and work well with others; and

(4) deal effectively with the demands and pressures of daily life and work. Emotional intelligence is a continuing process of developing specific emotional skills. Personal awareness, understanding, and meaning are at the heart of developing emotional skills, emotional learning, and emotional intelligence.

THE EMOTIONAL SKILLS ASSESSMENT PROCESS

A skill is a learned behavior that you choose to use to do your best in a specific situation. An intentional behavior is one that is chosen consciously, as opposed to a behavior that is impulsive or automatic. A person who behaves intentionally is an actor, not a reactor. Emotionally intelligent students act on their learning environment in self-directed ways—they do not react to it.

The ESAP covers four competency areas: Interpersonal, Leadership, Self-Management, and Intrapersonal. Each competency area includes particular emotional intelligence skills. Chapters 3 through 6 discuss the skills related to each area and provide you with an opportunity to assess your current level on each skill. After completing each skill assessment, your score is recorded on the Emotional Skills Profile—there is a graph for each skill as it is discussed and a complete profile in Chapter 7.

Essential Competency Areas and Related Skills

Action goal setting is a unique and important human ability to improve performance and structure change in healthy and successful ways. This ability enables you to learn and choose new feelings, thoughts, and behaviors that will improve personal satisfaction, success, and happiness. Research has shown that an emotionally intelligent student understands, possesses, and uses a set of 13 specific skills that can be classified into four competency areas.

PART I

Interpersonal Skills

Assertion is the ability to clearly and honestly communicate personal thoughts and feelings to another person in a comfortable, direct, appropriate, and straightforward manner. Assertive communication is a positive way of talking to people and expressing thoughts and feelings in a way that promotes understanding, caring, and respect. A person who communicates assertively respects the rights of others and does not hurt Self or others. Assertion enables a person to communicate effectively—even during difficult situations involving strong and intense emotions. It is an essential emotional skill for developing and maintaining strong, positive, and healthy relationships.

Potential Problem Areas

Aggression is the degree to which an individual employs a personal communication style or pattern that violates, overpowers, dominates, or discredits another person's rights, thoughts, feelings, or behaviors. It is reflected by communication that is too strong and overpowering, and it results in bad feelings and negative outcomes. Aggression is a potential problem area that negatively affects relationships. It involves the anger emotion, which must be understood and converted to the *Anger Management* emotional skill.

Deference is the degree to which an individual employs a communication style or pattern that is indirect, self-inhibiting, self-denying, and ineffectual for the accurate expression of thoughts, feelings, or behaviors. It is reflected by communications that are weak, indirect, or ambiguous and convey unclear or mixed messages. Often, Deference results in ineffective communications that negatively affect relationships. It involves the fear emotion, which must be understood and converted to the *Anxiety Management* emotional skill. Anxiety Management is essential to the healthy and constructive expression of fear, worry, and anxiety to Self and others.

PART II

Leadership Skills

Social Awareness or Comfort is the ability to choose the appropriate emotional, social, and physical distance during verbal and nonverbal interactions with others and to affect and influence others in positive ways. It includes establishing rapport and developing trust in relationships with others by using effective attending skills and by being honest, self-assured, and open. Social Awareness enables a person to be confident, spontaneous, and relaxed with others in a variety of situations. It is an essential emotional skill for developing and maintaining positive relationships with others.

Empathy is the ability to accurately understand and constructively respond to the expressed feelings, thoughts, behaviors, and needs of others. It involves actively listening in a patient, compassionate, and nonjudgmental manner and communicating back to the speaker that he or she has been heard, understood, and accepted as a person. Empathy allows a person to be viewed as caring, genuine, and trustworthy. It is an essential emotional skill for developing and maintaining positive relationships with others.

Decision Making is the ability to plan, formulate, initiate, and implement effective problem-solving or conflict-resolution procedures to resolve personal problems and to use a skills approach when making decisions. The skills include knowing about and using a systematic process daily to anticipate and resolve problems and make decisions. Decision Making is an essential emotional skill for formulating and acknowledging choice alternatives during problem situations and for involving others in the problem-solving or conflict-resolution process.

Positive Influence is the ability to positively affect, persuade, and influence others and to make a positive difference. It is a behavioral reflection of self-empowerment with developed interpersonal and goal-directed abilities and skills. Positive Influence is a set of personal and goal-directed behaviors and actions that create momentum, consensus, and support when working with others. It is an essential emotional skill for establishing and providing vision, momentum, and direction for others in ways that are valued and respected.

PART III

Self-Management Skills

Drive Strength is the ability to effectively direct personal energy and motivation to achieve personal, career, and life goals. It is reflected by meaningful goal achievement that results in personal satisfaction and positive feelings. Drive Strength involves learning specific strategies and action processes that can be applied and practiced on a daily basis in all areas of life. It is an essential emotional skill for high performance, goal achievement, and success.

Commitment Ethic is the ability to complete tasks, projects, assignments, and personal responsibilities in a dependable and successful manner, even under difficult circumstances. It is reflected by an inner-directed, self-motivated, and persistent effort to complete projects, regardless of other distractions or difficulties. Commitment Ethic involves a personal standard for meeting the goals, expectations, and requirements of life. It is an essential emotional skill for success and satisfaction and is the inseparable companion of high achievement and personal excellence.

Time Management is the ability to organize tasks into a personally productive time schedule and use time effectively to complete tasks. It is reflected by the ability to achieve and productively manage the valuable resource of time instead of responding or reacting to the demands of time. Time Management involves learning and using effective skills and bringing harmony to thoughts, feelings, and behaviors on a daily basis while pursuing personal, career, and life goals. It is an essential emotional skill for effective self-management.

Potential Problem Area

Change Orientation is the degree to which an individual is or is not satisfied and the magnitude of change necessary or desired to develop personal and professional effectiveness. It includes the degree to which a person is motivated and ready for change. Often, a high measure of Change Orientation is an indication of dissatisfaction with current personal and emotional skills and abilities, an acute interest in making personal changes, or a strong belief in the need to make personal changes. Change Orientation must be understood and converted to the *Positive Change* emotional skill. Positive Change is an essential emotional skill for healthy change and development throughout life.

PART IV

Intrapersonal Skills

Self-Esteem is the ability to view Self as positive, competent, and successful. It is reflected by genuine self-confidence, a high regard for Self and others, and self-worth. Positive Self-Esteem is the foundation for achievement and a general sense of well-being. It includes a powerful personal belief system about Self, personal competence, and self-value. Self-Esteem is developed and maintained when one experiences success when effectively dealing with Self, others, and the demands of life. It is an essential emotional skill for learning about and developing Self in all aspects of life.

Stress Management is the ability to choose and exercise healthy self-control and self-management in response to stressful events. It is reflected by the ability to control and manage the stress and strong emotions that arise daily during stressful situations. Stress Management involves the self-regulation of emotional intensity and the use of relaxation and cognitively derived coping strategies during difficult, high-stress situations. It is an essential emotional skill for health, performance, and satisfaction.

Self-Science Curriculum

To help people make positive personal changes, we encourage them to develop their own Self-Science Curriculum, or plan of action. We encourage them to adopt the view of a "personal scientist." A scientist approaches a problem as a challenge that requires precise effort and study. A scientist recognizes that it may take many attempts before finding a successful solution. Each attempt is viewed as a valuable learning experience to better guide the next experiment, not as a worthless failure.

When designing your Self-Science Curriculum, it is important to keep in mind that success and failure are not opposites; rather, they are closely related processes that are inherent in emotional learning. To experience success more often, a person may "fail" or may make many attempts. This is particularly true when attempting to reach high levels of success. Changing attitudes and behaviors while developing emotional intelligence is a process, not a single event.

Learning emotional intelligence is a focused and lifelong process of developing and improving specific emotional skills. Self-Science requires a safe, caring environment in which to learn, practice, and improve. As Self-Science activities and lessons are completed, people learn that achieving excellence requires self-defined and self-directed plans of action.

The ESAP connects the design of a Self-Science Curriculum with a learning process to develop emotional intelligence. The assessment process helps "personal scientists" objectively and accurately to view themselves in relation to Self and others; express and handle their emotions; and balance, harmonize, and manage their attitudes and behaviors. Positive emotional development is a major concern of everyone and a core value of successful organizations. We have learned from research, focused study, and experience that emotional intelligence is the most important factor to your success, performance, satisfaction, and happiness in life and work. The ESAP is a proven model to help make positive emotional development a priority . . . before something goes wrong.

Emotional Learning as Self-Science—Honest and positive assessment is at the heart of learning and developing emotional intelligence and creating positive ways to change.

DARWIN NELSON AND GARY LOW

LINK

Key factors in academic and career excellence include your ability to establish and maintain healthy and supportive relationships. These relationships are a major source of personal satisfaction and serve as an effective buffer to stress. Assertive communication skills and the ability to effectively manage and express strong emotions are essential to maintaining positive relationships. Your Emotional Skills Assessment Process (ESAP) begins in Chapter 3 with the Interpersonal competency area and the Assertion, Anger Management, and Anxiety Management skills. For a quick review, read Exhibit 2.8 to see what *EI Man* says about emotional intelligence!

EXHIBIT 2.8	WHAT IS EMOTIONAL INTELLIGENCE?

First of all, what are emotions? Simply put, emotions are your feelings. Sometimes you are happy, sometimes you are sad, or worried or puzzled or "at your wit's end." Sometimes you just don't care. There are lots of different emotions, but they are all combinations of the four basic emotions, which are:

HAPPY   SAD   ANGRY   AFRAID

Happy: you feel good, joyful, energetic, ready to go and "in tune with the world."
Sad: you feel down, depressed, jealous, full of grief, and "nobody cares about you."
Angry: you are mad, frustrated, irritable, grouchy and feel like the world "better shape up."
Afraid: you feel fear, anxiety, worry, guilt, paranoia and want to hide from life.

Second, what is Emotional Intelligence? It is investigating your emotions to find out if you are in control of them or are they in control of you? Next, you take your emotions and make them work for you as positive emotional skills and also improve possible emotional problem areas.

Positive emotional skills are:

1. **Interpersonal skills:**
   - **ASSERTION**—sticking up for yourself when you need to, directly and positively.

2. **Leadership skills:**
   - **COMFORT**—understanding the people around you so they will trust you.
   - **EMPATHY**—feeling what other people feel, and putting yourself in their shoes.
   - **DECISION MAKING**—planning ahead, thinking things through and making solid decisions to change or create a situation or solve a problem.
   - **LEADERSHIP**—being thoughtful and persuasive to positively influence other people.

3. **Self-management skills:**
   - **DRIVE STRENGTH**—being able to finish what you start, whatever it takes.
   - **TIME MANAGEMENT**—being able to manage time rather than it managing you.
   - **COMMITMENT ETHIC**—making a pledge to yourself to see things through to the end.

4. **Intrapersonal skills:**
   - **SELF-ESTEEM**—feeling that you have what it takes to "take care of business."
   - **STRESS MANAGEMENT**—being able to take the pressure and make things work well.

Potential problem areas are:

   - **AGGRESSION**—solving your problems with others by losing your temper and conflicting with them.
   - **DEFERENCE**—giving in to others because you don't want to assert yourself positively.
   - **CHANGE ORIENTATION**—being "stuck in a rut" instead of "going with the flow."

ACADEMIC AND CAREER SUCCESS PLANNER ACTIVITIES

Throughout the remainder of the text, each chapter will end with activities to help you develop specific EI behaviors for high achievement in college and career. The activities were borrowed from our Academic Success Planner (Nelson & Low, 2005, EI Learning Systems, Inc.) and are incorporated here because of their success and popularity on a variety of college campuses for developing EI Centric behaviors. Once you become familiar with the Academic and Career Success Planner Activities, use them daily to:

- Intelligently guide yourself though successful college and career experiences
- Plan, organize, and prioritize academic and personal obligations for each semester or season
- Identify and increase academic and career success behaviors
- Better understand how your emotions help or hinder your achievement
- Set and achieve daily goals that are important and satisfying to you
- Identify and effectively use your primary learning style for higher achievement
- Better manage stress
- Keep yourself on the path of high achievement and career success

ACTIVITY 2.1	IDENTIFYING YOUR LEARNING STYLE

VISUAL COGNITIVE	**VISUAL IMAGERY**	**AUDITORY**	**TACTILE KINESTHETIC**
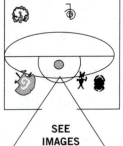	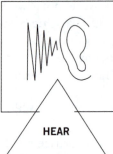	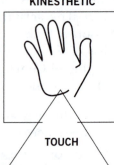	
SEE WORDS	**SEE IMAGES**	**HEAR**	**TOUCH**
• Written Text • Read • Write It!	• Pictures/Symbols • Visualize • Picture It!	• Spoken Words • Listen • Hear It!	• Movements • Action • Do It! Feel It!

BEST CLASSROOM LEARNING ENVIRONMENT

• Professor uses blackboard or overhead transparencies to list important facts • Provides outline of lecture/text materials • Benefit from text/class notes • Tend to study alone in a quiet room • Can see information in mind's eye	• Learn best when information is presented visually—picture/design format • Learn best from professor who uses visual aids, films, videos, maps, and charts • Tend to study alone in a quiet room • Remember by visualizing picture of concept in mind's eye • May have artistic side/visual arts	• Learn best by listening to oral presentation/lecture • Benefit from group discussion • Listen best interacting with others listening/speaking dialog • Benefit from study reviews using audio tapes	• Learn best when physically engaged—hands on! • Benefit from lab/field experience where you can be physically active • Benefit from professor who conducts in-class demonstrations, field trips, active, experienced-based learning

BEST LEARNING STRATEGIES

• Use color coding when studying new information • Prepare written summaries of key information • Make color-coded flashcards to be memorized • Write out key phrases and sentences to understand technical information • Maximize use of computer word processing • Use Post-it Notes for reminders	• Translate words/ideas to symbols/pictures • Make flash cards with symbols/pictures to aid memory • Use mind mapping for lecture/text note taking • Draw boxes in series to see step-by-step processes • Use computer word processing to create tables/charts • Use spreadsheets	• Establish a learning partnership/discuss with a friend/classmate • Join/develop a study/discussion group • When studying alone, talk out loud to aid recall/read aloud • Record lectures • Use Walkman for exam review • Talk yourself through difficult material	• In lecture classes, sit in front and actively take notes • Invent your own shorthand to jot down key words/concepts • Use mind maps/draw diagrams • Study moving with textbook, notes, flash cards in hand • Use Walkman for exam review

ACTIVITY 2.2	WHAT IS YOUR FAVORITE UNIVERSITY COLOR?

Graduation ceremonies are colorful and festive occasions, with many colors displayed on regalia from the academic disciplines represented in the ceremony. Find your favorite color on the chart below. Is this your major?

University Colors

Each academic discipline is represented by a specific color. Find your favorite color (discipline). Explore majors and related careers (Use the Occupation Outlook Handbook online). Use the Career Counseling Services on campus.

Agriculture: Maize
Arts/Letters/Humanities: White
Commerce/Accounting/Business: Drab
Dentistry: Lilac
Economics: Copper
Education: Light Blue
Engineering: Orange
Fine Arts/Architecture: Brown
Forestry: Russet
Journalism: Crimson
Law: Purple
Library Science: Lemon
Medicine: Green
Music: Pink
Nursing: Apricot
Oratory: Silver Gray
Pharmacy: Olive Green
Philosophy: Dark Blue
Physical Education: Sage Green
Public Administration/Foreign Service: Peacock Blue
Science: Golden Yellow
Social Work: Citron
Theology: Scarlet
Veterinary Science: Gray

CHAPTER 3

Interpersonal Skills

ASSERTION AND ANGER AND ANXIETY MANAGEMENT

To demonstrate some of the emotional skills, learning community students organized a volleyball game. The English 0301 students were informed that they would be writing about the activity after participating in two games. A young Afro-American male, who had not previously deemed himself assertive, displayed outstanding leadership and organizational skills over the course of the two games. He calmly managed the relationships in his team, and he communicated to his teammates with clear, non-aggressive instructions the mechanics of the game. He led his team to victory in both games. In a response paper about the volleyball experience, his peers noted his ability to relate constructively to his team members and to organize his team for success.

BEVERLY GAMMILL
English Instructor and EI Coordinator
Galveston College, Galveston, Texas

Preview

T his chapter begins the discussion of the four competency areas and the skills related to each area. A major factor in personal satisfaction, academic achievement, and career success is your ability and willingness to establish and maintain healthy interpersonal relationships. Your interactions and associations with others form an important part of the Emotional Intelligence (EI) curriculum. Friends, peers, teachers, mentors, and professional helpers can have a powerful influence on your academic and career development. The quality of your interpersonal relationships, especially with significant others in the school, career, and life contexts, affects your ability to focus on and complete meaningful academic and career goals.

The ability to act wisely in human relationships is interpersonal competence. Interpersonal competence requires that you apply and model three important emotional intelligence skills. Effective communication (the EI skill of Assertion) and emotional self-control (the EI skills of Anger and Anxiety Management), as well as understanding and appreciating the differences in others, are reflections of interpersonal intelligence. These communication and relationship skills allow you to work effectively in groups and teams.

As you work through and complete this chapter and the ones that follow, remind yourself that emotional intelligence skills are intentional habits—not fixed traits. Each chapter is a structured self-directed process to help you explore, identify, understand, learn, and apply and model specific emotional intelligence skills. As an emotionally intelligent student, you know that personal, academic, and career excellence results from lifelong learning and positive change.

This chapter begins by exploring the Assertion skill. Two potential problem areas—Aggression and Deference—and the applicable emotional intelligence skills are discussed next. Each section, in this chapter and Chapters 4 through 6, follows the same format: a discussion of the skill, an Emotional Intelligence Lesson, and an exercise.

ASSERTION

Cognitive Focus: Learning how and when to say what you really think and feel
Emotional Focus: Learning how to feel better when communicating with others
Action Focus: Choosing how you communicate when under stress

Definition

Assertive communication is the ability to clearly and honestly communicate your thoughts and feelings to others in a straightforward and direct manner. It is a way of talking to people that lets you express your thoughts and feelings

I. INTERPERSONAL SKILLS
Assertion

Assertion is the ability to communicate with others in a straightforward, direct, comfortable and respectful way.

You're not afraid to say what you need to say to somebody else, but you do it in a way that tells them you mean business but you respect their right to hear what you have to say in a fair but firm manner. You show you care both for what needs to get done and the person who is going to do it.

> ASSERTIVE PEOPLE ARE REASONABLE AND DIRECT. THEY ARE CALM IN STRESSFUL SITUATIONS. THEY REALIZE THAT PEOPLE NEED TO BE TREATED EQUITABLY AND FORTHRIGHTLY.

in a way that is not hurtful. Assertive communication allows you to respect your rights and the rights of others and is essential if you are to constructively express and deal with strong emotions like anger, fear, and sadness. To see how *EI Man* defines Assertion, look at Exhibit 3.1.

As you begin the "Step A. Self-Assessment: Explore" portion of each lesson, remind yourself to be totally honest and objective. This is not a test; there are no right or wrong answers. You may want to respond to each statement from a particular context (academic, career, relationships, family). Refer back to Exhibit 2.3, the Emotional Learning System, often to help make the process more intentional and natural.

EMOTIONAL INTELLIGENCE LESSON 1: ASSERTION

STEP A

Self-Assessment: Explore

Read each statement, determine whether the statement applies to you Most Often (M), Sometimes (S), or Least Often (L), and circle the applicable letter–number combination.

1. **Situation:** When I am really angry at someone, **I usually feel** some tension, but I am comfortable expressing exactly what is on my mind.　　M=2 S=1 L=0

2. When I am really angry at someone, **I usually think,** "OK, I'm angry and need to deal with it constructively." — M=2 S=1 L=0

3. When I am really angry at someone, **I usually behave** by expressing what is bothering me and working to achieve a constructive solution. — M=2 S=1 L=0

4. **Situation:** When someone is really angry at me, **I usually feel** tension and a right to understand the person's anger by responding directly. — M=2 S=1 L=0

5. When someone is really angry at me, **I usually think** that I have a right need to understand the person's anger at me and to respond directly to resolve the conflict. — M=2 S=1 L=0

6. When someone is really angry at me, **I usually behave** by asking for an explanation of the anger and by dealing with the feelings in a straightforward manner. — M=2 S=1 L=0

7. **Situation:** When I communicate with an "authority" person, **I usually feel** that my needs are legitimate and I am comfortable expressing exactly what is on my mind. — M=2 S=1 L=0

8. When I communicate with an "authority" person, **I usually think** that my needs are legitimate and that I should express them in a straightforward manner. — M=2 S=1 L=0

9. When I communicate with an "authority" person, **I usually behave** comfortably and easily with the person. — M=2 S=1 L=0

10. **Situation:** When a person makes an important request of me, I **usually feel** comfortable saying either "yes" or "no" to the request. — M=2 S=1 L=0

11. When a person makes an important request of me, **I usually think** that I have the right to say "yes" or "no" and feel comfortable with either response. — M=2 S=1 L=0

12. When a person makes an important request of me, **I usually behave** according to my true feelings at the time and comfortably tell the person either "yes" or "no." — M=2 S=1 L=0

13. **Situation:** When I make an important request of a person, **I usually feel** confident and comfortable about my right to make the request. — M=2 S=1 L=0

14. When I make an important request of a person, **I usually think** that I have a right to make the request and will respect the person's decision about how to respond. — M=2 S=1 L=0

15. When I make an important request of a person, **I usually behave** comfortably and straightforwardly while making the request. — M=2 S=1 L=0

16. **Situation:** When I am around a new group of people, **I usually feel** a little uneasy, but comfortable. — M=2 S=1 L=0

17. When I am around a new group of people, **I usually think** that I will have fun meeting them and that I want some of them to know me. — M=2 S=1 L=0

18. When I am around a new group of people, **I usually behave** in a relaxed manner by introducing myself to someone who looks interesting or by visiting around.

M=2 S=1 L=0

Stop and add your score. *(Max. score = 36)*   **TOTAL SCORE** _____

Transfer your score to the graph in Step B and to the appropriate profile on pages 173–174.

STEP B

Self-Awareness: Identify

Communication is especially difficult under stressful conditions. Assertion is a powerful emotional skill that helps you communicate more effectively, honestly, and appropriately.

9 12 15 18	21 24 27	30 33 36
DEVELOP	STRENGTHEN	ENHANCE
You can benefit from learning about and understanding the Assertion skill. Work through the lesson to fully develop this important interpersonal communication and relationship skill.	You currently identify the Assertion skill as one that is at an average level of development. You can improve this skill and make it a strength.	You are claiming the Assertion skill as a current strength. Find ways to refine and enhance this important skill.

STEP C

Self-Knowledge: Understand

The ability to communicate honestly and in a way that demonstrates respect is the key to developing and maintaining healthy and productive interpersonal relationships. Most people can speak well and communicate effectively with friends and colleagues in situations that are relaxed, informal, and comfortable. However, other situations are not so easy. Many people experience difficulty when speaking in more formal settings. In awkward, unfamiliar, or stressful situations, it is common for people to be anxious, make mistakes, be misunderstood, or just not perform well. Positive communication builds and strengthens relationships; negative communication creates problems and can destroy relationships. Assertion is an emotional skill that is essential to positive communication and confidence.

EXHIBIT 3.2	THE COMMUNICATION CONTINUUM

Communication Continuum

Deference	Assertion	Aggression

Deference: Potential Problem Area

                                   Aggression: Potential Problem Area

                    Assertion: Skill Area

Assertive communication skills are essential in relationships, especially ones that are important or intimate. Assertive communication is a learned skill and an alternative to using "old" brain (automatic) verbal responses in stressful or difficult situations. If you do not learn this communication skill, you have only two ways to respond to others when you experience strong emotions—with aggression or with deference. In a stressful or difficult situation, the automatic or conditioned emotional responses are anger and fear. These emotions trigger verbal responses that are aggressive or deferring. An aggressive response is hurtful to the other person. A deferring response is hurtful to you, and the other person never knows what you really think or feel.

People often hesitate to tell others what they really think and feel because they do not know how to express themselves without hurting the feelings of others. When you allow your real thoughts and feelings to stack up inside, you can become anxious, depressed, or angry. Assertive communication is a valuable skill because it provides a way for you to express your feelings constructively and consistently. Refer to Exhibit 3.2, The Communication Continuum, to see better how the communication patterns relate to one another. The goal for communication is to learn to communicate in a perfectly assertive way in every situation.

STEP D

Self-Development: Learn

Communicating assertively requires that you keep in mind your rights as a person, as well as the rights of the person to whom you are speaking. You have the right to say what you think and feel about any situation, and you want to do so in a way that respects the other person's right to disagree with or be different from you. How you say something is as important as the actual words that you use to send your message.

When communicating assertively, try to use the first-person singular pronoun *I*. This indicates that you accept responsibility for the thought or feeling expressed and that it is yours. *I think, I feel*, and *I believe* are the starting points for an assertive response. The second part of an assertive statement describes the event or situation that is connected to your thought or feeling and describes it clearly—*I feel angry when you yell at me for making a mistake.* The third part of an assertive response lets the other person know what you want to have happen instead of what is currently the case—*I feel angry when you yell at me for making a mistake, and I would prefer that we discuss the problem and focus on how to solve it.*

Learning Assertion requires understanding that communication occurs with another person—a friend, family member, professor, supervisor, or someone you do not know. This person is different from you in some way, and it is essential that you be able to communicate effectively with a wide range of people. Managing diversity issues with respect and skill is critical to academic and career success. To fully develop the emotional intelligence skill of Assertion, you must learn how to skillfully deal with the cognitive, emotional, and action (behavioral) components of wise or emotionally intelligent behavior.

Communication occurs with another person and in a specific context. When there is an extra level of pressure and stress involved and when the situation is important to you, communication is more difficult. A higher level of skill is required because of the degree of difficulty and stress. Identify a situation that you should address to improve your communication abilities. Develop this situation into a brief scenario, and describe it in the space provided. An example is provided to get you started.

> I am worried about my grade in rhetoric and composition. My assignments are confusing, and I don't understand them. If I do not change something, I may make a bad grade. What can I do?

YOUR SCENARIO: _____

_____

_____

_____

| STEP E |

Self-Improvement: Apply and Model

Intentionally applying and modeling assertive behaviors on a daily basis is a reflection of emotional intelligence. Wisdom unites knowledge and behavior,

and assertion is a key skill. Think of how your academic performance and career outlook might be improved by consistently applying and modeling this
skill. Consider the following list of assertive behaviors that you can apply and
model. Add others as you reflect on assertion and discover how assertion can
help you.

- Scheduling an appointment with a professor to discuss and clarify a
  term paper assignment.
- Setting up a quiet time study schedule with my roommates for midse-
  mester exams.
- Calling my parents to let them know that I have to cut the holidays
  short to complete some difficult course requirements.
- Calling about and setting up tutorial services to help me improve my
  writing skills.
- Completing the required work that I had been avoiding before spring
  break.

Learning to communicate assertively takes work and practice because it is
a completely new way to talk to others. Practice assertive communication
with yourself and in groups. Brainstorm additional exercises to improve your
assertiveness skills.

EXERCISE

Complete the following exercise and use it as you develop the Assertion emotional skill into an intentional habit.

A. EXPLORE   How do you think, feel, and behave when you use this skill?

Cognitive Focus. Learning how and when to say what you really think and feel

_____

_____

_____

Emotional Focus. Learning how to feel better when communicating with others

_____

_____

_____

Action Focus. Choosing how you communicate when under stress

_____

_____

_____

B. IDENTIFY   Provide your personal definition of Assertion.

_____

_____

_____

_____

_____

C. UNDERSTAND   Describe the importance of Assertion.

_____

_____

BENEFITS:

_____

_____

D. LEARN   Describe how to learn Assertion.

_____

_____

_____

_____

_____

E. APPLY AND MODEL   List ways to practice.

_____

_____

_____

_____

_____

Potential Problem Areas: Aggression and Deference

Anyone can become angry—that is easy. But to be angry with the right person, to the right degree, at the right time, for the right purpose, and in the right way—this is not easy.

ARISTOTLE

This section discusses communication patterns and personal communication styles that arise when a person is in a stressful situation. Remember that automatic and out-of-awareness thinking can trigger emotionally reactive behavior. We have all had the experience of hearing ourselves say something and then wish we had not. Not one of us is healthy enough to behave perfectly, and we can learn to use reflective thinking to express ourselves better in difficult situations.

The focus of this section is on managing strong negative emotions, especially anger and fear. The proving ground for your ability to communicate assertively, to effectively express anger, and to overcome your negative emotionally reactive habits is within your relationships with significant and important others. How you communicate affects productivity, as well as the quality and longevity of your important relationships.

Aggression and deference become problematic when what you say is emotionally reactive or determined—it is not guided by reflective thought. All of us have emotionally responsive "buttons" that someone or something can push and cause us to feel anger, fear, or sadness. Assertive skills enable us to anticipate potential problems and effectively communicate in stressful situations.

Reflective Thinking and Emotional Expression

Our automatic reactions and interpretation of external and internal events can create the strong and powerful emotions of anger and fear. Such reactive behaviors can occur without a conscious awareness of the thoughts underlying the emotion, and they often result in conflict. It is important to learn and remember that these emotionally quick responses often create more difficult problems. It is essential to develop a more reflective and skilled response.

If you explore the components of an emotional experience, you find a series of interrelated sequences: (a) the perception of an event, (b) the automatic interpretation of the event, (c) the interpretation of your response, and (d) the specific emotional outcomes of anger, fear, sadness, or joy. Learn and remember what happens when emotions are negative and reactive.

The anger emotion makes attacking behaviors easier. Anger is closely connected to the thought that someone has done something bad and deserves punishment. The unique thing about anger is that everything that comes afterward makes it more intense. Angry words (Aggression) increase your anger and can damage yourself and others.

Fear helps you escape from threatening situations and keeps you safe from danger. Physical threat is different from psychological threat. You defer in your communication when you think that what you say will hurt another person's feelings or when you are afraid of the other person's reactions. In either case, your communication is inhibited or restricted in ways that lead to deferring communication patterns (this is called Deference).

Assertive communication is based on reflective thinking and a consideration for the personal rights of Self and others. Assertive communication is powerful and respectful. To develop assertion as a primary communication style, you must learn to identify and express anger and fear honestly, directly, and appropriately. Anger Management and Anxiety Management are essential emotional intelligence skills that contribute to assertive communication.

ANGER MANAGEMENT

Cognitive Focus: Managing anger to say what you really think and feel
Emotional Focus: Feeling better about dealing with anger
Action Focus: Choosing assertion in stressful situations.

Definition

Anger Management is the ability to express anger constructively in relationship to Self and others. *Aggression* is the degree to which an individual employs a personal communication style or pattern that violates, overpowers, dominates, or discredits another person's rights, thoughts, feelings, or behaviors. Aggression is a potential problem area that negatively affects relationships and must be converted to the *Anger Management* emotional skill. To see *EI Man's* take on aggressive communication patterns, have a look at Exhibit 3.3, the Potential Problem Area of Aggression.

EXHIBIT 3.3	POTENTIAL PROBLEM AREA: AGGRESSION

POTENTIAL PROBLEM AREAS
Aggression

Do you resolve your differences with other people by getting angry, yelling and screaming or maybe even fighting? Do you like to dominate or overpower others to get your way? Being too aggressive is not a good way to have positive relations with people. If the answers are yes, you need to work on Anger Control and Management. And also ask yourself: "Does being really mad make you feel good?" Bet it doesn't.

AGGRESSION: CONFLICT, HOSTILITY, COMBAT AND THE LIKE VERY SELDOM RESOLVE ANY ISSUES IN THE LONG RUN. GENERALLY THEY JUST LEAD TO MORE OF THE SAME. HISTORY IS FULL OF EXAMPLES OF THIS.

EMOTIONAL INTELLIGENCE LESSON 2: ANGER MANAGEMENT

Self-Assessment: Explore

Read each statement, determine whether the statement applies to you Most Often (M), Sometimes (S), or Least Often (L), and circle the applicable letter–number combination.

1. **Situation:** When I am really angry at someone, **I usually feel** hostile or the need to verbally attack.   M=2 S=1 L=0

2. When I am really angry at someone, **I usually think** to attack and powerfully show my anger.   M=2 S=1 L=0

3. When I am really angry at someone, **I usually behave** by angrily expressing myself or getting into an argument.   M=2 S=1 L=0

4. **Situation:** When someone is really angry at me, **I usually feel** angry and hostile and the need to attack.   M=2 S=1 L=0

5. When someone is really angry at me, **I usually think** that I must respond even stronger so I am not overwhelmed.   M=2 S=1 L=0

6. When someone is really angry at me, **I usually behave** by showing my own anger or escalating the fight.   M=2 S=1 L=0

7. **Situation:** When I communicate with an "authority" person, **I usually feel** defensive or the need to develop a strategy for my approach to the person.   M=2 S=1 L=0

8. When I communicate with an "authority" person, **I usually think** that what I want or need is more important and impose myself on the person.   M=2 S=1 L=0

9. When I communicate with an "authority" person, **I usually behave** in a pushy or defensive manner toward the person.   M=2 S=1 L=0

10. **Situation:** When a person makes an important request of me, **I usually feel** resentment or upset that the person expects a "yes."   M=2 S=1 L=0

11. When a person makes an important request of me, **I usually think** that I don't like the imposition and usually say "no" even if I feel otherwise.   M=2 S=1 L=0

12. When a person makes an important request of me, **I usually behave** defensively and say "no" or grudgingly let the person know that I resent the request.   M=2 S=1 L=0

13. **Situation:** When I make an important request of a person, **I usually feel** determined about getting what I want and not concerned with the person's feelings.   M=2 S=1 L=0

14. When I make an important request of a person, **I usually think** that what I need or want is important and that the person should respond immediately.   M=2 S=1 L=0

15. When I make an important request of a person, **I usually behave** in a   M=2 S=1 L=0
pushy and sometimes overpowering manner while making the request.

16. **Situation:** When I am around a new group of people, **I usually feel**   M=2 S=1 L=0
uncomfortable or pressured to get a conversation going, even if I have
to be a little pushy.

17. When I am around a new group of people, **I usually think** that I must   M=2 S=1 L=0
get things started whether the others are ready or not.

18. When I am around a new group of people, **I usually behave** by talking   M=2 S=1 L=0
too much, or I often come on too strong.

Stop and add your score. *(Max. score = 36)*   **TOTAL SCORE** _____

Transfer your score to the graph in Step B and to the appropriate profile on pages 173–174.

STEP B

Self-Awareness: Identify

Communication is especially difficult under stressful conditions. Aggression
is a pattern of communication that must be converted to the powerful, emotional skill of Anger Management.

2 4 6	8 11 15	19 24 28 35
LOW	NORMAL	HIGH
A low score on Aggression is positive. This means that you are claiming Anger Management as a current strength. Continue to find ways to refine and enhance the Anger Management skill.	You currently identify the Anger Management skill as one that is at an average level of development. You can improve this skill and make it a strength.	A high score on Aggression indicates a potential problem area. You can benefit from learning and improving the Anger Management skill. Work through the lesson to fully develop the important interpersonal communication and relationship skill of Anger Management.

STEP C

Self-Knowledge: Understand

If you are to express anger constructively, you have to recognize anger when it
occurs and identify the emotion accurately. Anger is a normal human emotion,

and everyone experiences it. Anger is self-defeating and damaging when you use the emotion to hurt yourself or others.

When you learn to identify anger accurately and exercise control over how to deal with its intensity, duration, and expression, your mental and physical health improve. Learning to control and express anger is one of the most important skills you can learn and practice in your daily life.

A person who does not learn the skill of anger control may feel out of control. In fact, many people use anger to explain their behavior—"Why did you drink too much and wreck your car?" "I was angry at my wife;" "Why did you say all those horrible things?" "She made me mad." Many people blame others for their anger and avoid their responsibility for dealing with or managing their emotions.

Anger and its related behaviors of psychological and physical violence are major problems in our society today. On an individual level, uncontrolled anger shortens our life and damages its quality, as well as our relationships with others. When we learn to recognize anger and exercise a choice over how we want to express it, our lives improve and we benefit psychologically and physically.

STEP D

Self-Development: Learn

The first step in controlling anger is to learn how to identify the emotion accurately. To do this, you must make the distinction between a thought, a feeling, and a behavior. Frustration and jealousy are thoughts. Anger is the emotion. Psychological abuse and violence are behaviors.

Three intense emotions cause problems: anguish, anger, and fear. Anguish is the emotion people call sadness or depression, and it is caused by emotional thoughts about the past. Anger occurs in the present and is caused by angry thoughts about what is happening or not happening. Fear is the emotion people call anxiety, tension, worry, and confusion, and it is a result of thinking about the future and worrying that bad things will happen. Before you can control anger, you must be able to identify it correctly. "I am angry!!"

To practice and learn anger control, follow the steps in Exhibit 3.4. Remember, your goal is to recognize anger and then express it constructively so as not to do damage to yourself or others.

If you are experiencing intense anger, you cannot think. If you start expressing the anger without thought, each angry thing you do or say increases and escalates the anger to rage. Use the process from Exhibit 3.4 each time you experience anger.

EXHIBIT 3.4	ANGER CONTROL

STEP 1. When you experience frustration, annoyance, jealousy, say to yourself, *"I am angry."*

STEP 2. Once you have accurately identified the emotion, say to yourself, *"I create my own anger"* (i.e., I am creating my anger with angry thinking).

STEP 3. After you have realized that you are making yourself angry, say, *"I accept responsibility for my anger."*

STEP 4. Next, ask yourself, *"How do I want to express this anger in a way that I feel good about?"*

STEP 5. Ask yourself whether you need help from another person. If you are really angry, you should take a time-out—leave the anger-producing situation, take a walk, and give yourself time to think about what you want to do or say.

STEP E

Self-Improvement: Apply and Model

Aggression is an indication of the degree to which a person employs a personal communication style that is too strong for healthy and productive relationships. Depending on the degree of aggression, this style may overpower, violate, or discredit the other person's thoughts, feelings, or behaviors. A high score may indicate insensitivity toward others and a lack of respect.

The intensity of anger can increase rapidly and often leads us to say things or do things that we later regret. We may become verbally or physically violent as our anger escalates into rage. When we experience intense or extremely high levels of anger, it is almost impossible to think and act productively. We become a part of the anger, and one angry behavior leads to another.

To break the escalating cycle of anger, you must learn specific skills to control and manage yourself. One skill that you can practice is the Time-Out. By learning to use and practice Time-Out, you will be able to moderate your anger before it reaches an intense level. When you become angry, the key is to manage yourself and take action that will allow you to better control your thoughts and behaviors. It is impossible to think constructively when you are feeling intense anger.

The Time-Out skill requires that you immediately remove yourself from the anger-producing situation. This action prevents your anger from reaching the irrational or rage level and gives you time to rethink the situation and de-cide how you want to handle yourself.

It is important to remember that taking a Time-Out is something that you want to do to better manage your anger. You leave the situation because you choose to, not because you cannot handle what is happening. You are not walking away from a difficult situation. You are leaving the scene to allow the intensity of your anger to subside, collect your thoughts, and decide on the best possible way to approach the problem.

The Time-Out is put into effect when you say to yourself or to the others involved, *"I'm beginning to feel angry and I want to take a time-out."* This state-ment is clear and assertive. The first part is an "I" statement that indicates you are talking about yourself, not blaming the others for your anger. The next part accurately identifies your emotion and describes what is happening. The last part is a direct communication about your choice of how you want to be-have now. The purpose of the statement is to acknowledge that you are mak-ing a choice about how best to deal with your anger. This builds feelings of self-confidence and self-control. After making the statement, follow the re-maining steps in Exhibit 3.5.

In some situations, your anger will be too intense to work through in one or two hours. You may take several days to think through an anger-producing situation involving an important person. You may have strong feelings

EXHIBIT 3.5	TIME-OUT

STEP 1. Leave the situation for a definite period of time, such as one hour. If an-other person is involved, explain how the time-out works and what you are doing. Tell the person when you will be back.

STEP 2. Do something physical such as going for a walk, working in the garage, jog-ging, or exercising briefly. The activity should be something that will work for you, but must also be constructive—do not drink or take drugs.

STEP 3. Think about how you want to handle the situation. Brainstorm options and rehearse what you will say and do.

STEP 4. After sufficient time has passed, check your anger level. If you have thought through the situation and want to discuss it, let the other person know you are willing to talk about the problem. If your anger starts to escalate when you think about the situation, repeat the time-out procedure. Let the other person know that you need additional time to calm yourself and agree on a time to discuss the problem.

because the situation and the other person are important to you. Give yourself time and permission to cope with the problem.

Time-Outs help rebuild trust in relationships that have been damaged by anger and destructive behavior. When others see you working to express and deal with your anger constructively, they know that you are putting time and energy into making the relationship better. Be patient and practice.

EXERCISE

Complete the following exercise and use it as you develop the Anger Management emotional skill into an intentional habit.

A. EXPLORE   How do you think, feel, and behave when you use this skill?

Cognitive Focus. Learning how and when to say what you really think and feel

_____

_____

_____

Emotional Focus. Learning how to feel better when communicating with others

_____

_____

_____

Action Focus. Choosing how you communicate when under stress

_____

_____

_____

B. IDENTIFY   Provide your personal definition of Anger Management.

_____

_____

_____

C. UNDERSTAND   Describe the importance of Anger Management.

_____

_____

BENEFITS:

_____

_____

_____

D. LEARN Describe how to learn Anger Management.

_____

_____

_____

_____

E. APPLY AND MODEL List ways to practice.

_____

_____

_____

_____

ANXIETY MANAGEMENT

Cognitive Focus: Managing anxiety so I can say what I really think and feel
Emotional Focus: Feeling better about dealing with fear
Action Focus: Choosing assertion in stressful situations

Definition

Anxiety Management is the ability to manage self-imposed anxiety (fear) and effectively communicate with others. _Deference_ is the degree to which an individual employs a communication style or pattern that is indirect, self-inhibiting, self-denying, and ineffectual for the accurate expression of thoughts, feelings, or behaviors. It involves the fear emotion that must be understood and converted to the _Anxiety Management_ emotional skill. Changing how you communicate during stressful (anxiety-producing) situations is a major personal change that can bring you many emotional benefits. _EI Man's_ discussion of Deference and Anxiety Management is provided in Exhibit 3.6, Potential Problem Area: Deference.

Reasons Why People Act Nonassertively

Although there are many reasons why people do not express assertive behaviors, the following are some of the primary reasons:

■ Confusing firm assertion with aggression
■ Confusing deference with politeness

EXHIBIT 3.6	POTENTIAL PROBLEM AREA: DEFERENCE

Deference

Are you shy and timid and let other people run over you very easily because you are afraid they will be angry with you and won't like you? Do you not say what you really think because you feel if you do, there will be problems? If so, then you need to work on Fear Control and Management to learn how to be Assertive when you need to.

> A PERSON WHO IS HUMBLE USUALLY WORKS QUITE WELL WITH OTHER PEOPLE. BUT IF HUMILITY GOES TOO FAR AND A PERSON BECOMES TOO DEFERENTIAL, IT CRIPPLES THEIR ABILITY TO BE EFFECTIVE; IT MAKES THEM A SHEEP TO BE PUSHED AROUND BY WHOEVER FEELS LIKE IT.

- Mistaking deference for being helpful
- Failing to accept personal rights
- Having a deficit in skills

EMOTIONAL INTELLIGENCE LESSON 3:
ANXIETY MANAGEMENT

STEP A

Self-Assessment: Explore

Read each statement, determine whether the statement applies to you Most Often (M), Sometimes (S), or Least Often (L), and circle the applicable letter–number combination.

1. **Situation:** When I am really angry at someone, **I usually feel** anxious or confused about what to say. M=2 S=1 L=0

2. When I am really angry at someone, **I usually think** that I should not express my anger directly. M=2 S=1 L=0

3. When I am really angry at someone, **I usually behave** by not saying anything to the person so as not to hurt the person's feelings. M=2 S=1 L=0

4. **Situation:** When someone is really angry at me, **I usually feel** confused and afraid or the need to avoid the person. M=2 S=1 L=0

5. When someone is really angry at me, **I usually think** that I am probably at fault or that the person does not like me.   M=2 S=1 L=0

6. When someone is really angry at me, **I usually behave** by backing off, apologizing, or not really saying what I feel.   M=2 S=1 L=0

7. **Situation:** When I communicate with an "authority" person, **I usually feel** nervous and hesitant about approaching the person.   M=2 S=1 L=0

8. When I communicate with an "authority" person, **I usually think** that I really shouldn't bother the person or take up too much time.   M=2 S=1 L=0

9. When I communicate with an "authority" person, **I usually behave** apologetically and awkwardly toward the person.   M=2 S=1 L=0

10. **Situation:** When a person makes an important request of me, **I usually feel** uncomfortable saying "yes" or "no" to the request.   M=2 S=1 L=0

11. When a person makes an important request of me, **I usually feel** nervous or anxious about refusing the request.   M=2 S=1 L=0

12. When a person makes an important request of me, **I usually behave** in the way the person wants or refuse and apologize for my response.   M=2 S=1 L=0

13. **Situation:** When I make an important request of a person, **I usually feel** anxious or reluctant about approaching the person.   M=2 S=1 L=0

14. When I make an important request of a person, **I usually think** that I really should not be imposing on or bothering the person.   M=2 S=1 L=0

15. When I make an important request of a person, **I usually behave** hesitantly or awkwardly while making the request.   M=2 S=1 L=0

16. **Situation:** When I am around a new group of people, **I usually feel** anxious or confused about how to start a conversation.   M=2 S=1 L=0

17. When I am around a new group of people, **I usually think** that they are more relaxed than I am or that I don't have much to say.   M=2 S=1 L=0

18. When I am around a new group of people, **I usually behave** cautiously and wait until someone comes to talk to me.   M=2 S=1 L=0

Stop and add your score. (*Max. score = 36*)   **TOTAL SCORE** _____

Transfer your score to the graph in Step B and to the appropriate profile on pages 173–174.

STEP B

Self-Awareness: Identify

Communication is especially difficult under stressful conditions. Deference is a pattern of communication that must be converted to the powerful emotional skill of Anxiety Management.

2 4 6 10	14 18 22	26 30 32 36
LOW	STRENGTHEN	HIGH
A low score on Deference is positive. This means you are claiming Anxiety Management as a current strength. Continue to find ways to refine and enhance the Anxiety Management skill.	You currently identify the Anxiety Management skill as one that is at an average level of development. You can improve this skill and make it a strength.	A high score on Deference indicates a potential problem area. You can benefit from learning and improving the Anxiety Management skill. Work through the lesson to fully develop the important interpersonal communication and relationship skill of Anxiety Management.

STEP C

Self-Knowledge: Understand

Changing your primary communication style from deference to assertion improves your self-esteem, your important relationships with others, and your ability to positively manage stress. Most people who use the deference communication style score high in feeling sensitivity (empathy) and are very kind and polite people. A deferring person is often sensitive and does not want to say things that are hurtful or painful to others. Although empathy is a strength, what must be changed is how and what you say. Assertive communication allows you to maintain your sensitivity while still being true to your own thoughts and feelings.

STEP D

Self-Development: Learn

How you communicate depends on the situation. Use the following guide to learn the process of changing your communication style. Describe a recent incident or situation where you deferred to someone else. Be specific.

When did it start?

_____

_____

How often does it occur?

_____

_____

Under what conditions?

_____

_____

Who is present?

_____

_____

What happens just prior?

_____

_____

What happens afterward?

_____

_____

What are your feelings about your nonassertive behavior in this situation?

_____

_____

How could you act more assertively?

_____

_____

Predict the outcome of your assertive behavior.

_____

_____

STEP E

Self-Improvement: Apply and Model

Complete the following exercises to practice using the various types of assertive behaviors.

1. Basic assertion. This is a simple expression of standing up for one's rights, feelings, or beliefs. Some cases of basic assertion involve expressing appreciation toward other people.

Example: I appreciate your good work.

PRACTICE: _____

_____

2. Empathic assertion. This type of assertion involves making a statement that has two parts: conveying recognition of the other person's situation or feelings and expressing your own thoughts and observations.

Example: I understand how important this is to you, and I am not comfortable doing what you have asked.

PRACTICE: _____

_____

3. Confrontational assertion. This is used when the other person's words contradict his deeds. This type of assertion involves three parts: recalling what the other person said he would do, objectively describing what the other person actually did do, and expressing what you'd like to see happen or what you want. The entire assertion is said in a matter-of-fact, nonjudgmental manner.

Example: You said you would phone if you were delayed. You did not call. I would like to be able to count on your call so that I know that you are safe.

PRACTICE: _____

_____

The following are a few suggestions of areas for continued practice. Brainstorm other situations to add to the list.

- Dealing with my fear of making an oral presentation and asking for help in preparing for it.
- Coming to grips with my uncertainty about a major and scheduling time for career counseling.
- Exploring my negative feelings about the class and deciding to withdraw rather than settling for a mediocre grade.
- Developing my computer skills at the university lab instead of remaining confused about how to do an Internet search.
- Confronting my uptight exam behavior and attending a skills training seminar on managing test anxiety.

Now that you understand the difference between assertive communication (the skill) and deference (a style or pattern of response), you can see and feel the value of true assertive communication. An important by-product of assertive communication is increased self-confidence.

No one can make you feel inferior without your consent.

ELEANOR ROOSEVELT

EXERCISE

Complete the following exercise and use it as you develop the Anxiety Management emotional skill into an intentional habit.

A. EXPLORE   How do you think, feel, and behave when you use this skill?

_____

_____

_____

Cognitive Focus: Managing anxiety so that I can say what I really think and feel

_____

_____

Emotional Focus: Feeling better about dealing with fear

_____

_____

_____

Action Focus: Choosing assertion when in stressful situations

_____

_____

_____

B. IDENTIFY   Provide your personal definition of Anxiety Management.

_____

_____

C. UNDERSTAND   Describe the importance of Anxiety Management.

BENEFITS:

D. LEARN   Describe how to learn Anxiety Management.

E. APPLY AND MODEL   List ways to practice.

WHEN EMOTIONS ARE NEGATIVE

The primary human emotions are anger, fear, sadness, and happiness. At the survival or emergency level, anger helps us fight, fear helps us flee, and sadness helps us let go or disengage. Happiness helps us engage and enjoy the present. Emotions are negative only when their intensity and duration damage our or another person's physical or emotional health, disrupt our important relationships, decrease our productivity and performance, or interfere with our levels of academic and career achievements.

It is important to understand your interpersonal communication skills and recognize how the emotions of anger and fear contribute to the aggression and deference styles. Because aggression and deference are emotionally reactive behaviors and seemingly automatic, it is essential to identify the primary and secondary communication styles that you use when under stress. Otherwise, it is difficult to pinpoint what you need to change and how to improve your interpersonal relationships.

To better understand how you communicate in difficult or stressful situations, review the scores from the three Emotional Intelligence Lessons in this chapter. Most people use all three communication styles to some extent in every communication with others. Your highest score on these three scales indicates your primary communication pattern. The second highest score indicates your secondary or backup style. Develop a graph comparing your scores in these three areas. Rank them as first, second, or third.

ASSERTION		
9 12 15 18	21 24 27	30 33 36
AGGRESSION		
2 4 6	8 11 15	19 24 28 35
DEFERENCE		
2 4 6 10	14 18 22	26 30 32 36

If your highest score is Assertion, that is your primary communication style when under stress. This indicates that you tend to use a direct, honest, and appropriate expression of thoughts, feelings, and behaviors when communicating with others. A high (primary) score in either Aggression or Deference may indicate a lack of communication skills or the need to adjust them. An effective assertion style is important for healthy interaction with others. An excess of either aggression or deference in interpersonal communication negatively affects your interactions and gives rise to self-defeating behaviors.

The emotionally intelligent student knows about the importance of language and that what you say influences your interpretation of events and situations. How you talk to yourself (self-talk) and others (interpersonal communication) influences the intensity of your emotionally reactive responses and often results in negative and unwanted consequences.

LINK

In the next chapter, you will learn the important Leadership emotional skills of Social Awareness, Empathy, Decision Making, and Positive Influence. Emotionally intelligent behavior is essential for wide-ranging and successful interactions with others. These skills will help you with complex diversity issues and provide you with a foundation for improving your people skills and leadership abilities.

Academic and Career Success
Planner Activities

Balanced Academic Schedule

MWF Classes	TTh Classes	Other Classes
1._____	1._____	1._____
2._____	2._____	2._____
3._____	3._____	3._____
4._____	4._____	4._____

College Contacts

Professor_____
Class_____
Office Hours_____
Building_____
Room_____Phone_____
E-mail_____

Professor_____
Class_____
Office Hours_____
Building_____
Room_____Phone_____
E-mail_____

Professor_____
Class_____
Office Hours_____
Building_____
Room_____Phone_____
E-mail_____

Professor_____
Class_____
Office Hours_____
Building_____
Room_____Phone_____
E-mail_____

Professor_____
Class_____
Office Hours_____
Building_____
Room_____Phone_____
E-mail_____

Professor_____
Class_____
Office Hours_____
Building_____
Room_____Phone_____
E-mail_____

ACTIVITY 3.2	THE ASSERTION CALENDAR FOR HIGHER PERSONAL ACHIEVEMENT

Month_____ Year_____

El Skills Focus:

Assertion

Communicating and behaving in honest and direct ways. Active in seeking out resources and assistance to improve academic achievements and personal performance,

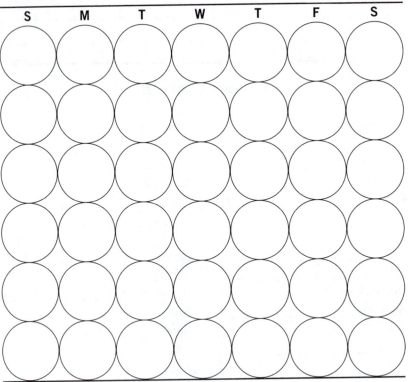

S	M	T	W	T	F	S

Will Do Behaviors: Assertion

Priority	When	Target Date
1._____	1._____	1._____
2._____	2._____	2._____
3._____	3._____	3._____
How important?	How urgent?	Completion Date

ACTIVITY 3.3	THE ACADEMIC BEHAVIOR CHECKLIST

Academic Behavior Checklist

Read each statement and check the appropriate box. Zero if you never do it, "1" if you sometimes do it, or "2" if you always do it. Be thoughtful and honest. Total your score to see how many learning behaviors you share with high achieving college students. Find and mark, or circle your score on the chart.

	Never	Sometimes	Always
1. Organize my personal and academic responsibilities into an efficient schedule.			
2. Write down important personal goals to be completed at a certain time.			
3. Set, write down, and complete important personal goals daily.			
4. Arrive for class prepared and on time.			
5. Get assignments and obligations completed on time.			
6. Complete responsibilities and assignments in spite of personal difficulties.			
7. Motivate myself with challenging personal goals.			
8. Improve my level of achievement by learning new skills.			
9. Study and read for many more hours than I actually spend attending required class meetings.			
10. Effectively deal with emotions and work through personal problems and obstacles.			
11. Believe in my ability to succeed and do not give up on myself.			
12. Focus on success more than failure.			
13. Play and have fun in healthy ways.			
14. Effectively regulate and express the strong emotions of anger, fear, and sadness.			
15. Maintain/improve personal wellness by exercise, adequate sleep, and nutrition.			
16. Avoid self-destructive behaviors and relax naturally.			
17. Go to sleep easy after long and difficult days.			
18. Actively involve myself in organizations or special interest groups I like.			
19. Actively form positive, supportive, and collaborative relationships with classmates.			
20. Seek out friends, family members, and others who support and encourage my success.			
21. Learn from more academically capable friends, mentors, or tutors.			
22. Know, locate and use campus learning resources to improve and learn new skills.			
23. Organize and participate in study support groups to complete class assignments.			
24. Identify, maximize, and apply personal learning style strengths to improve achievement.			
25. Accept personal responsibility for motivation, achievement, and happiness.			
26. Commit to learning as my primary career.			
27. Ask questions and share ideas with classmates.			
28. Seek help when I need it.			
29. Seek out and get feedback from instructor to clarify and better understand assignments.			
30. Attend all required classes.			
31. Focus on personal strengths (i.e., hard worker) and improve weaknesses (i.e., computer skills).			
32. Monitor (watch), record, and change self-defeating and nonproductive behaviors.			
33. Turn in written assignments after a first draft, review and revision, and final edit.			
34. Create and control a personal and effective study place that is comfortable for me.			
35. Feel in control of personal responsibilities and academic demands.			
36. Do not procrastinate and waste time.			

Where are you now? Which behaviors do you need to increase? Who can help you most?

2 4 6 8 10 12 14 16 18 20 22 24 26 28 30 32 34 36 38 40 42 44 46 48 50 52 54 56 58 60 62 64 66 68 70 72
   Low Achieving   Successfully Achieving   High Achieving

Use this Academic Success Planner to increase important behaviors, set specific personal goals, and improve academic achievement. Record your daily scale and monitor your progress weekly.

ACTIVITY 3.4 | ASSERTIVE BEHAVIORS FOR HIGH ACHIEVEMENT

Assertive Academic Behaviors

YES=1   NO=0

In class, with classmates, and on campus, DO YOU:

_____Introduce yourself to the professor using your preferred name.

_____Use the professor's preferred name/title.

_____Find out about course requirements and instructors' teaching styles before class meets.

_____Find out and record each professor's office location and office hours.

_____Know how best to contact your professors: by phone, fax, e-mail, or appointment.

_____Attend each class prepared with required text.

_____Be alive, engaged, and participate actively in class.

_____Identify and maximize your personal learning style (auditory, kinesthetic, visual, tactile).

_____Discuss, dialog, and disagree with respect.

_____Ask questions, share ideas, and talk with classmates.

_____Form learning partnerships with classmates you respect.

_____Actively ask and seek help from classmates, professors, mentors, and tutors.

_____Take notes, create mind-maps, highlight during class.

_____Join/form a study/learning group that meets at designated times.

_____Accept personal responsibility for motivation and learning.

_____Contact and inform professors about missing required classes.

_____Inform instructor and college when dropping a class.

_____Use Internet, library, mentors, tutors, and special resources for learning.

_____Demonstrate genuine interest in learning by being involved.

_____Ask for and go find help when it is needed.

_____Get a head start on difficult classes by preparing before signing up.

_____**Total Score**

Be actively engaged in learning by using campus resources to improve your skills.

Active

21
19
17
15
13
11
9
7
5
3
1

Reactive

ACTIVITY 3.5	THE ASSERTION MAP FOR HIGHER PERSONAL ACHIEVEMENT

Assertion Map

I accept responsibility for my success.

High achieving students are active and self-directed rather than reactive and other-directed. Practice identifying and changing nonassertive situations into opportunities for you to apply assertive behaviors to improve your academic achievement and personal satisfaction.

1. List a nonassertive situation to change;
   i.e., confused about a class assignment.

   1._____
   _____

2. State the desired assertive behavior;
   i.e., contact professor to discuss and clarify.

   2._____
   _____

3. State when, where, how, and what you did;
   i.e., called professor, set appointment;
   discussed, clarified assignment.

   3._____
   _____

4. State results/benefits. Did you do the
   behavior? If not, why not?
   i.e., given clear understanding
   of assignment.

   4._____
   _____

5. Identify thoughts and feelings after
   successfully completing the behavior;
   i.e., I am clear about what to do and feel
   more confident.

   5._____
   _____

Positive Assertive Behaviors:

List five activities (behaviors) that you can do to create positive feelings for yourself.

Examples:

Watching a favorite video. Being a good friend. Calling a family member. Visiting a favorite place. Playing a game.

_____   _____

_____   _____

_____   Do one of these behaviors after you
                              have done something you had to do.

CHAPTER 4

Leadership Skills

SOCIAL AWARENESS, EMPATHY, DECISION MAKING, AND POSITIVE INFLUENCE

Since the first grade my daughter had been told she couldn't. Through her participation in the learning community and work on her Emotional Intelligence skills, she now is confident that she can succeed. She is happy with her accomplishments and the leadership skills she is developing.

PARENT OF COLLEGE STUDENT
Galveston College

Preview

E ffective leadership is people centered, and effective leaders know, understand, and respect the needs, values, and goals of others. A genuine respect for the differences in others and the ability to communicate and accurately understand the differing points of view are the essence of emotionally intelligent leadership.

The ability to quickly establish and comfortably maintain effective interpersonal relationships with a wide range of individuals and groups reflects the Social Awareness emotional intelligence skill. The ability to accurately understand and accept differing viewpoints requires the skill of Empathy. The Social Awareness and Empathy skills are interdependent and necessitate an assertive communication style.

Reasoning and emotions are interactive and both are essential for effective Decision Making and person-centered leadership. Intuitive wisdom, a major contribution of the emotional mind, influences your decision-making ability and provides the energy and stamina that move you toward your goals. Remember, deciding is a process, not an event. When you have a decision that you cannot "make," talk it out, get feedback, and pay attention to your emotions and let them help unlock your cognitive thoughts.

One view of decision making is that it should be separated from emotions and be a completely logical and rational process. A similar view perceives good leaders as people with a particular collection of stable traits or personal characteristics. When these views are personalized as negative belief systems, you might hear such statements as, "I cannot make a decision" and "I have never been a leader and never will be." These are isolated views of the cognitive system.

Emotions are the key to creative problem solving. The initiative- and goal-directed component of Positive Influence is also a contribution of the emotional mind. When you apply the Positive Influence skill, you act more than you react, and you accept responsibility for achieving your academic and career goals.

Meaningful relationships are hard to find if you "look" for them, and they are sometimes slow to develop if you wait for them to happen. Without healthy and supportive connections with others, our personal resources are often inadequate in times of high stress. Actively seek out relationships with people who are genuinely interested in your success, care what happens to you, and will help you when you honestly need help.

SOCIAL AWARENESS

Cognitive Focus: Learning to listen to and hear others
Emotional Focus: Learning how to feel more comfortable relating to others
Action Focus: Choosing how to initiate and build comfortable relationships

Definition

Social Awareness is a by-product of interpersonal awareness and our actual behavior when relating to others. It is the ability to affect others positively

EXHIBIT 4.1	EI SKILL: SOCIAL AWARENESS AND COMFORT

II. LEADERSHIP SKILLS
Comfort

A positive leader is socially aware, and feels the emotional needs of the people who work around her. She shows them that she truly understands her co-workers, so that she has their trust and cooperation and they know that it is not necessary to put up and hide behind any kind of protective walls. Basically she makes them feel comfortable with her and the work they do for her, which makes for a beneficial workplace for everybody.

> TO MAKE PEOPLE FEEL COMFORTABLE, A LEADER NEEDS TO HAVE THEIR TRUST AND RESPECT, SHE DOES THIS BY BEING HONEST, SELF-ASSURED AND OPEN WITH THEM.

and develop trust and rapport in relationships. Social Awareness is a result of attending behaviors that are both verbal and nonverbal. Rapport is achieved through good eye contact, a pleasant greeting, and a willingness to self-disclose (say something about yourself to the other person). Active listening is the best way to make a good, comfortable contact with another person—a willingness to attend to what another person is saying (pay attention) and letting that person know that you have heard the message sent. Social Awareness enables a person to be confident, spontaneous, and relaxed with others in a variety of situations. In Exhibit 4.1, *EI Man* explains Social Awareness and Leadership in terms of comfort, which is how Social Awareness is assessed on the Emotional Skills Assessment Process (ESAP).

EMOTIONAL INTELLIGENCE LESSON 4: SOCIAL AWARENESS

STEP A

Self-Assessment: Explore

Read each statement, determine whether the statement applies to you Most Often (M), Sometimes (S), or Least Often (L), and circle the applicable letter–number combination.

1. My voice is variable and clear, and I am easily heard by others.   M=2 S=1 L=0
2. My relationships with others are smooth and comfortable.   M=2 S=1 L=0

3. I am confident in my ability to be comfortable and effective when communicating with others.   M=2 S=1 L=0

4. I know when to talk and when to listen.   M=2 S=1 L=0

5. My ability to use my whole body (e.g., eyes, facial expressions, tone, and touch) makes communicating with others easy for me.   M=2 S=1 L=0

6. I know how to ask for a favor without imposing.   M=2 S=1 L=0

7. My handshake is confident and firm and communicates a solid feeling about myself to others.   M=2 S=1 L=0

8. I know how close I can be to a person without making that person feel uncomfortable.   M=2 S=1 L=0

9. I can tell how friendly I can be with a stranger.   M=2 S=1 L=0

10. I can determine whether I can introduce myself or should wait to be introduced.   M=2 S=1 L=0

11. I am comfortable with all kinds of people.   M=2 S=1 L=0

12. I know when it is okay for me to put my hand on another person's shoulders.   M=2 S=1 L=0

Stop and add your score. *(Max. score = 24)*   **TOTAL SCORE** _____

Transfer your score to the graph in Step B and to the appropriate profile on pages 173–174.

STEP B

Self-Awareness: Identify

Social Awareness is a leadership skill that enables you to positively lead and work well with others. Effective leaders learn and develop appropriate social skills.

5 7 9 11 13	15 17 19	21 23 24
DEVELOP	STRENGTHEN	ENHANCE
You can benefit from learning about and understanding the Social Awareness skill. Work through the lesson to fully develop this important leadership skill.	You currently identify the Social Awareness skill as one that is at an average level of development. You can improve this skill and make it a strength.	You are claiming the Social Awareness skill as a current strength. Continue to find ways to refine and enhance this important skill.

STEP C

Self-Knowledge: Understand

Relationships are the source of much satisfaction or dissatisfaction in our lives. Establishing rapport by practicing active listening helps us initiate and maintain healthy relationships with others. We spend many hours learning to speak and write correctly and very little time learning how to listen and how to communicate understanding to another person. Good relationships do not just happen. A good relationship with another person is built, and rapport is an important skill to give a relationship an opportunity to fully develop.

One of the best feelings a person can have is being listened to by a person who is interested. The type of listening being described is called active because it requires that heightened attention, concentration, and awareness are focused on the other person. During active listening, you selectively attend to the other person's words and feelings and pay more attention to the other person than to your own thoughts or interpretations about what the person is saying. The goal is to really hear what the other person is saying and to let that person know that she has been heard by your response.

STEP D

Self-Development: Learn

Active listening is an important skill to develop to accurately understand what others are saying. The most important part of active listening is to state in your own words (paraphrase) what you have just heard the speaker say. Do not repeat the sender's words verbatim. Use feedback in the form of a question to check your understanding of what you have heard. Ask the speaker to tell you more about any message that you do not clearly receive. Ask the speaker to verify that you have heard the message accurately (cross-checking).

STEP E

Self-Improvement: Apply and Model

Practice active listening when you are in a group, in counseling sessions, in relationships with significant others, or when you want to be helpful to others. When listening actively, ensure that you:

- Make eye contact and attend to the speaker to indicate your interest in the person.
- Make a conscious decision not to interpret, judge, or advise the speaker.

- Put aside your own thoughts and ideas by really focusing on what the other person is saying.
- Rephrase the message you heard in your own words and ask whether you heard and understood the message correctly to correct errors and misunderstandings.
- Use questions to clarify any message that is not understood to verify and validate the message.

A person who has developed the Social Awareness skill is able to:

- Initiate and establish relationships that encourage success.
- Feel comfortable asking others for help when necessary.
- Actively establish relationships with mentors.
- Meet and have friendships with many different people.
- Keep relationships comfortable.

EXERCISE

Complete the following exercise and use it as you develop the Social Awareness emotional skill into an intentional habit.

A. EXPLORE   How do you think, feel, and behave when you use this skill?

_____

_____

_____

Cognitive Focus: Learning to listen to and hear others

_____

_____

Emotional Focus: Learning how to feel more comfortable relating to others

_____

_____

Action Focus: Choosing how to initiate and build comfortable relationships

_____

_____

B. IDENTIFY   Provide your personal definition of Social Awareness.

_____

_____

_____

_____

_____

C. UNDERSTAND   Describe the importance of Social Awareness.

_____

_____

BENEFITS:

_____

_____

D. LEARN   Describe how to learn Social Awareness.

_____

_____

_____

_____

_____

E. APPLY AND MODEL   List ways to practice.

_____

_____

_____

_____

_____

EMPATHY

Cognitive Focus: Learning to listen to and hear others

Emotional Focus: Feeling better about accurately understanding others

Action Focus: Choosing better responses to communicate understanding

EXHIBIT 4.2	EI SKILL: EMPATHY

Empathy

Empathy is the state of mind that allows you to understand and feel what other people feel.

An empathic person is a good listener, is patient and compassionate and is open-minded and nonjudgmental.

A person capable of true empathy communicates this in a caring, friendly and easy-going manner to the other people that she associates with.

> O GREAT SPIRIT, GRANT THAT I SHOULD NOT CRITICIZE MY NEIGHBOR UNTIL I HAVE WALKED A MILE IN HIS MOCCASINS.
> NATIVE AMERICAN PROVERB

Definition

Empathy is the ability to accurately understand and constructively respond to the expressed feelings, thoughts, and needs of others. Accurate Empathy involves communicating to the sender that he or she has been heard, understood, and accepted as a person. Empathy is a process of letting a person know that you have understood that person's feelings.

When you communicate assertively, your message is clear, honest, and direct. How you speak is important, and your ability to listen and accurately hear what someone else is saying and feeling is essential to establishing and maintaining effective relationships. Comfortable, healthy relationships are created between two people when the talk is straight, the listening is active, and the differences are recognized and appreciated. When you care about the other person and want to be helpful, accurate Empathy is important. *EI Man* says there is an old Native American Proverb that teaches the Emotional Intelligence (EI) skills of Empathy. Exhibit 4.2, Empathy, provides a little humor.

EMOTIONAL INTELLIGENCE LESSON 5: EMPATHY

STEP A

Self-Assessment: Explore

Read each statement, determine whether the statement applies to you Most Often (M), Sometimes (S), or Least Often (L), and circle the applicable letter–number combination.

1. I am a caring person, and people seem to sense this about me.   M=2 S=1 L=0

2. I understand and am patient with someone who is experiencing a lot of emotions.   M=2 S=1 L=0

3. I am a warm and accepting person, and people are comfortable talking to me about really private concerns and feelings.   M=2 S=1 L=0

4. I am the kind of person that people are really able to talk to about personal problems.   M=2 S=1 L=0

5. My friends tell me that I am an understanding person.   M=2 S=1 L=0

6. I feel the emotions of others as they feel them.   M=2 S=1 L=0

7. I listen to and really understand another person's feelings.   M=2 S=1 L=0

8. I am considered to be a good listener.   M=2 S=1 L=0

9. I accurately understand how a person feels when he is talking to me.   M=2 S=1 L=0

10. When someone is telling me something important, I concentrate on the person and really hear her.   M=2 S=1 L=0

11. I accurately feel what another person feels.   M=2 S=1 L=0

12. When another person tells me what he is feeling, I understand the feelings and really listen to him.   M=2 S=1 L=0

Stop and add your score. *(Max. score = 24)*   **TOTAL SCORE** _____

Transfer your score to the graph in Step B and to the appropriate profile on pages 173–174.

STEP B

Self-Awareness: Identify

Empathy is a leadership skill that enables you to positively lead and work well with others. Effective leaders accept and accurately understand others.

6 8 10 12 14	16 18 20	22 24
DEVELOP	STRENGTHEN	ENHANCE
You can benefit from learning about and understanding the Empathy skill. Work through the lesson to fully develop this important leadership skill.	You currently identify the Empathy skill as one that is at an average level of development. You can improve this skill and make it a strength.	You are claiming the Empathy skill as a current strength. Continue to find ways to refine and enhance this important skill.

STEP C

Self-Knowledge: Understand

Responding empathetically allows the sender of a message to feel understood and accepted on a personal level. Empathy is communication at a feeling level that is helpful and therapeutic (healing). It involves active listening with respect for the other person's thoughts and feelings. To communicate empathically, you have to put your view of the world aside and focus on the reality of things as seen by the speaker. The goal of Empathy is to let the person know that her thoughts and feelings are important to you—not because you agree—but because you respect her as a person different and separate from you.

Words like *trust*, *acceptance*, *caring*, and *respect* are used to describe healthy relationships. The feelings of comfort and safety that you feel in the relationship with your "best friend" are the result of the other person's ability to put himself aside and accept you as a person of value. Empathy is present in caring relationships, and it is essential that you practice this skill in your close relationships. Empathy occurs when you "step into the shoes" of another person and view the world through his or her eyes.

STEP D

Self-Development: Learn

Use the Empathy skill when you want to be of maximum help to another person. When another person is talking about how he or she feels, Empathy is the best way to respond. Empathic responding encompasses active listening and providing feedback. To develop Empathy skills, listen for feelings. Your empathic response should reflect back the feeling that you heard the other person express. The emotion expressed may be more important than just the idea conveyed by the words.

When practicing empathic responding, ask yourself what emotion the other person is feeling. Does the person feel happy, sad, angry, or afraid? Reflect back your perception of the other person's feelings. This helps the other person identify or become aware of the feeling. Do not be afraid to guess at the emotion you hear expressed. If you are wrong, the other person will tell you and further clarify the emotion being experienced.

When learning and practicing Empathy, you are learning to listen for feelings. Most conversations are carried out on two levels—the verbal or cognitive level and the emotional or feeling level. Practice your Empathy skills by listening for the emotion or feeling underlying the words spoken.

STEP E

Self-Improvement: Apply and Model

Following are four statements that people might make. Read each one and try to determine the feeling underlying the words. Using a single word or short phrase, identify the feelings that you think the statement conveys. Check your accuracy with your classmates or get feedback from friends.

1. My employees are always on my back with some kind of hassle, and I'm fed up with the whole deal.

   _____

2. I'm overloaded with work at the office and at home, and I can't handle it anymore. I don't know what to do.

   _____

3. I am trying my best, and everyone is telling me that I have to do more. I'm disappointed in myself and feel like a failure.

   _____

4. My boss has asked me to take on another project. I want to say yes, but I don't think I can take the extra stress.

   _____

   A person who has developed the Empathy skill is able to:

   ■ Practice active listening to really hear what another person is saying.
   ■ Be patient and understanding when another person is having strong feelings.
   ■ Accept differences in others, even when disagreeing with their ideas.
   ■ Have a good sense about what another person is feeling.
   ■ See things from the other person's point of view.
   ■ Communicate sensitivity and respect for the feelings of others.

EXERCISE

Complete the following exercise and use it as you develop the Empathy emotional skill into an intentional habit.

A. EXPLORE   How do you think, feel, and behave when you use this skill?

_____

_____

_____

Cognitive Focus: Learning to listen to and hear others

_____

_____

Emotional Focus: Feeling better about accurately understanding others

_____

_____

Action Focus: Choosing better responses to communicate understanding

_____

_____

B. IDENTIFY   Provide your personal definition of Empathy.

_____

_____

_____

_____

C. UNDERSTAND   Describe the importance of Empathy.

_____

_____

BENEFITS: _____

_____

D. LEARN   Describe how to learn Empathy.

_____

_____

_____

_____

_____

_____

E. APPLY AND MODEL   List ways to practice.

_____

_____

_____

_____

_____

DECISION MAKING

Cognitive Focus:	Resolving problems and conflicts
Emotional Focus:	Feeling good about personal choices
Action Focus:	Selecting a proactive strategy to solve problems

Definition

Decision Making is the ability to use effective problem-solving and conflict-resolution strategies to resolve issues. It requires using a systematic model to approach the problems that occur daily.

The ability to make quick decisions and demonstrate good judgment has an important emotional component. The experiential mind comes to the support of the cognitive mind when difficult problems require resolution and important decisions have to be made. Much has been said about how emotions interfere with reasoning, and more must be understood about how emotions spark creativity, curiosity, and intuition.

The experiential mind plays an extremely important role in shaping your fundamental values and your characteristic behaviors. Emotions are a source of energy for high performance, motivation, and innovation. In Exhibit 4.3 _EI Man_ says that Decision Making is both a science and an art!

EXHIBIT 4.3	EI SKILL: DECISION MAKING

Decision Making

To be able to make a good solid decision that will work, the decision maker needs to plan ahead, think things through, come up with new ideas if necessary and then, based on a thorough grasp of the situation, proceed to make and stick by that decision.

This requires a systematic approach to anticipating and solving problems and for formulating and acknowledging various choice alternatives required by that decision.

> MAKING AN EFFECTIVE, SOLID DECISION IS A SCIENCE AND AN ART. THINK IT OVER THOROUGHLY AND SET IT IN MOTION. IF IT WORKS, GREAT. IF NOT, BE BIG ENOUGH TO ADMIT IT'S WRONG AND YOU NEED TO TRY SOMETHING ELSE.

EMOTIONAL INTELLIGENCE LESSON 6: DECISION MAKING

STEP A

Self-Assessment: Explore

Read each statement, determine whether the statement applies to you Most Often (M), Sometimes (S), or Least Often (L), and circle the applicable letter–number combination.

1. I make a decision and act instead of worrying about possible alternatives and becoming tense. M=2 S=1 L=0

2. I make my decisions independently and rarely ask for help from supervisors, family, or associates. M=2 S=1 L=0

3. I follow an established process that guides me when making important decisions. M=2 S=1 L=0

4. When involved in a group project, I suggest solutions that other group members accept. M=2 S=1 L=0

5. I am a good decision maker. M=2 S=1 L=0

6. When faced with making an important decision, I can see several alternatives and make a decision based on priorities. M=2 S=1 L=0

7. My decisions are usually accepted as "good" by the people affected. M=2 S=1 L=0

8. My friends and coworkers ask for my help when making important decisions. M=2 S=1 L=0

9. I am decisive when a stressful situation calls for an immediate decision and action.　　　　　　　　　　　　M=2 S=1 L=0

10. I seldom regret the decisions that I have made.　　　　M=2 S=1 L=0

11. I make decisions easily and with good results.　　　　M=2 S=1 L=0

12. When faced with making an important decision, I am not overly anxious about making a wrong choice.　　　　M=2 S=1 L=0

Stop and add your score. *(Max. score = 24)*　　　**TOTAL SCORE** _____

Transfer your score to the graph in Step B and to the appropriate profile on pages 173–174.

STEP B

Self-Awareness: Identify

Decision Making is a leadership skill that enables you to positively lead and work well with others. Effective leaders make decisions and solve problems.

5 8 10 12	14 16 18	20 22 24
DEVELOP	STRENGTHEN	ENHANCE
You can benefit from learning about and understanding the Decision-Making skill. Work through the lesson to fully develop this important leadership skill.	You currently identify the Decision-Making skill as one that is at an average level of development. You can improve this skill and make it a strength.	You are claiming the Decision-Making skill as a current strength. Continue to find ways to refine and enhance this important skill.

STEP C

Self-Knowledge: Understand

Decision-Making and problem-solving skills are essential because our lives are never free of problems. In fact, the human brain has a tendency to create problems a little more rapidly than we can solve them. Most of us have the ability to create problems in our minds that have only negative resolution options. How we perceive problems is an important key to our ability to resolve them.

If problems are viewed as barriers or blocks, they can become a source of inconvenience, annoyance, and failure. If you view problems as those things that prevent you from having a happy and productive life, it indicates that your goal is to completely eliminate problems. Unfortunately, this is an impossible goal. A more constructive view is that problems exist for a purpose and that they present an opportunity to actively participate in life. Your goals should include actively confronting problems, working toward personally meaningful resolutions, and generating creative options to deal with problems as they arise.

STEP D

Self-Development: Learn

As you begin to learn Decision-Making and problem-solving skills, remember to define your problems in terms of ineffective solutions—not in terms of barriers or blocks to your happiness (impossible situations). The problem is not the problem. The problem is finding an effective solution that allows you to feel happier or better.

To develop a more effective approach to personal problem solving, use the following guidelines:

- Accept the fact that living means having problems and that it is possible to cope with most problem situations. Sharing problems instead of hiding or denying them is helpful in finding effective solutions.

- Recognize and identify problems as they occur. When you have an emotional response (e.g., anger, fear, sadness), take this as a clue to identify a problem area. Focus on the situation producing the emotional response—do not deny the feeling.

- Hold back your first impulse to respond or to do nothing at all. Your automatic response may not be the most effective.

STEP E

Self-Improvement: Apply and Model

To practice effective Decision Making, complete the following exercise. Select a problem that is important to you—pick one that requires an effective solution now. Share the problem that you are attempting to resolve with others and ask for feedback and suggestions. Then, answer each of the five questions.

1. Define your problem and state it specifically (e.g., controlling my anger).

---

2. Identify and outline your usual response in a specific situation (e.g., When my supervisor criticizes me, I get really angry and attack back).

_____

_____

_____

3. List at least three options or possible solutions (e.g., I could ignore the criticism, I could tell her what I think and feel about the criticism, I could take a time-out and think about what I want to do and say).

_____

_____

_____

4. Visualize the consequences of each of your three responses.

STRATEGY 1

POSITIVE CONSEQUENCES   NEGATIVE CONSEQUENCES

_____

_____

_____

STRATEGY 2

POSITIVE CONSEQUENCES   NEGATIVE CONSEQUENCES

_____

_____

_____

STRATEGY 3

POSITIVE CONSEQUENCES   NEGATIVE CONSEQUENCES

_____

_____

_____

5. Decide on the strategy with the best consequences, and evaluate your results.

Satisfactory _____ What happened? _____

Unsatisfactory _____ What happened? _____

When the problem occurs again, I have learned that:

_____

_____

and I will change my response by:

_____

_____

This is a systematic process for actively handling and resolving problems. You can return to this process many times as you encounter new problems. Learn to view problems as challenges and opportunities. Develop confidence and use a systematic, proactive process to respond to these challenges and opportunities.

EXERCISE

Complete the following exercise, and use it as you develop the Decision-Making emotional skill into an intentional habit.

A. EXPLORE   How do you think, feel, and behave when you use this skill?

_____

_____

_____

Cognitive Focus: Resolving problems and conflicts

_____

_____

_____

Emotional Focus: Feeling good about personal choices

_____

_____

_____

Action Focus: Selecting a proactive strategy to solve problems

_____

_____

_____

B. IDENTIFY   Provide your personal definition of Decision Making.

_____

_____

C. UNDERSTAND   Describe the importance of Decision Making.

BENEFITS:

D. LEARN   Describe how to learn Decision Making.

E. APPLY AND MODEL   List ways to practice.

POSITIVE INFLUENCE

Cognitive Focus: Positively affecting and influencing others

Emotional Focus: Feeling better about personal leadership

Action Focus: Using mentoring and coaching to provide positive influence

Definition

Positive Influence is a behavioral reflection of self-empowerment, interpersonal, and goal achievement skills. It is a set of personal and goal-directed behaviors that create consensus and momentum and gain the active support of

---

EXHIBIT 4.4	EI SKILL: LEADERSHIP

Leadership

Good leadership means to be able to be thoughtful and persuasive to give others a positive direction in which to go.

A good leader is thoughtful, firm but fair and gets people to follow him or her by helping everybody on the team understand that they are all working together.

This requires a set of personal and goal-directed actions that create momentum and consensus when working with others.

IT HAS OFTEN BEEN SAID THAT A TRULY GREAT LEADER IS ONE WHO KNOWS HOW TO FOLLOW AS WELL AS LEAD.

---

others. Positive Influence results from a self-directed, internal process that is grounded in positive self-esteem, guided by clear personal values, and observable in proactive, self-confident behaviors. It is a cumulative set of behaviors that are observed by others and evaluated as valuable and meaningful directions to follow.

You are an effective leader when your relationships with others are characterized by honesty, trust, empathy, integrity, dependability, and a respect for diversity. The energy, excitement, and commitment to a purpose necessary to develop these relationships come from the emotional mind. In a sense, Positive Influence is a process that reflects a person's ability to model emotionally intelligent behavior. A person demonstrates harmony (congruence) and wisdom (good judgment) by integrating the experiential and cognitive systems. *EI Man* provides an interesting view of Leadership in Exhibit 4.4.

Exhibit 4.5 is an emotional skills model for Positive Influence. As you can see, the Positive Influence skill is connected to many of the other important emotional intelligence skills and competency areas—it is an interactive set of skill behaviors. Effective leaders create a climate that facilitates Positive Influence by knowing, understanding, and respecting the needs, characteristics, values, and goals of others. Communicating respect and genuine caring to others is the essence of Positive Influence. When combined, these skills support the Leadership competency area.

Do not allow yourself to be led astray by a leader.   I CHING

EXHIBIT 4.5	POSITIVE INFLUENCE: AN EMOTIONAL SKILLS MODEL

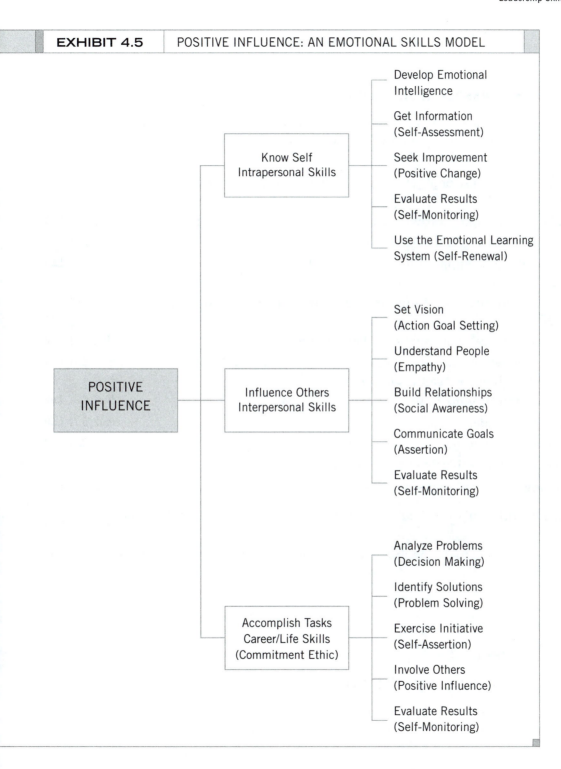

EMOTIONAL INTELLIGENCE LESSON 7: POSITIVE INFLUENCE

STEP A

Self-Assessment: Explore

Read each statement, determine whether the statement applies to you Most Often (M), Sometimes (S), or Least Often (L), and circle the applicable letter–number combination.

1. When I really feel strongly about something, I can influence a group to agree.   M=2 S=1 L=0

2. I make a strong and positive impact on most of the people I meet.   M=2 S=1 L=0

3. I am persuasive without taking advantage of others.   M=2 S=1 L=0

4. I feel comfortable approaching a person with the idea of selling her something.   M=2 S=1 L=0

5. When a group that I am in needs a spokesperson, I am usually elected.   M=2 S=1 L=0

6. I can "take charge" of a situation when required.   M=2 S=1 L=0

7. I am a convincing and believable person, and my friends often ask me to "talk to" someone for them.   M=2 S=1 L=0

8. My friends involve me in solving their problems.   M=2 S=1 L=0

9. I am a good leader.   M=2 S=1 L=0

10. I have an ability to help others solve problems.   M=2 S=1 L=0

11. I positively affect others just by being myself.   M=2 S=1 L=0

12. I put others at ease in tense situations.   M=2 S=1 L=0

Stop and add your score. (Max. score = 24)   **TOTAL SCORE** _____

Transfer your score to the graph in Step B and to the appropriate profile on pages 173–174.

STEP B

Self-Awareness: Identify

Positive Influence is a skill that enables you to positively lead and work well with others. Effective leaders influence others in positive ways.

4 6 9 11	13 15 17	19 21 24
DEVELOP	STRENGTHEN	ENHANCE
You can benefit from learning about and understanding the Positive Influence skill. Work through the lesson to fully develop this important skill.	You currently identify the Positive Influence skill as one that is at an average level of development. You can improve this skill and make it a strength.	You are claiming the Positive Influence skill as a current strength. Continue to find ways to refine and enhance this important skill.

STEP C

Self-Knowledge: Understand

As an emotional skill, Positive Influence means providing momentum and direction for others in ways that are valued and respected. Self-Esteem, Assertion, Empathy, and Positive Influence skills influence the emergence of leadership behaviors within us. Leading others to achieve positive and meaningful goals is a by-product of believing in ourselves, sharing our thoughts and feelings assertively, and taking the initial risk to move in personally valued directions.

Positive Influence is a highly valued and respected skill—manipulation and coercion are absent. One leads best by behavioral example. The results of Positive Influence are clear when the directions taken lead to an increase in achievement and satisfaction that benefits those who followed, as well as the one who led.

STEP D

Self-Development: Learn

Self-assertion is basic to leadership and necessary for self-empowerment. Assertive communication lets other people know how you think and feel. Self-assertion begins with claiming your power. As a person, you have basic rights. Following are a few rights that some people consider important in assertive communication. Review the list and discuss them with your classmates. Are you comfortable with these rights?

COMMUNICATION RIGHTS (ASSERTION)

- I have the right to say what I really think and feel about any issue.
- I have the right to disagree.

- I have the right to say "no" to a request that another person makes of me.
- I have the right to be angry and express it in a way that does not hurt me or anyone else.
- I have the right to ask for what I want.

Next, make a list of the personal rights that you want to claim when communicating with others. Leadership requires that you positively influence others—a process that begins only after you have claimed your strengths as a person and started to communicate with others in honest and direct ways.

Important personal rights that I want to remember when talking to others are:

_____

_____

_____

STEP E

Self-Improvement: Apply and Model

Positive Influence involves accepting responsibility for the things that you want to accomplish and doing what is right for you. Developing this ability also requires that you become active, not reactive, and develop your own vision (map).

Self-awareness, visioning, and action goal setting are key skills that allow us to create meaningful personal direction and stay true to the course we have chosen. Self-awareness allows us to plan our actions and develop proactive behaviors. Visualization taps our creative potential and forms a picture of what is possible. In his book *The 7 Habits of Highly Effective People: Powerful Lessons in Personal Change* (1989), Stephen Covey called this process "beginning with the end in mind."

Begin to practice the Leadership competency skills by developing a mission statement (a personal philosophy) that sets forth what you value and consider to be important behavioral guidelines. Develop a mission statement that is unique and meaningful to you. Include your most important beliefs and clearly state your personal mission. Use short declarative statements that you can control.

PERSONAL MISSION STATEMENT _____

_____

_____

_____

_____

EXERCISE

Complete the following exercise and use it as you develop the Positive Influence emotional skill into an intentional habit.

A. EXPLORE   How do you think, feel, and behave when you use this skill?

_____

_____

_____

_____

Cognitive Focus: Positively affecting and influencing others

_____

_____

_____

Emotional Focus: Feeling better about personal leadership

_____

_____

_____

Action Focus: Using mentoring and coaching to provide positive influence

_____

_____

_____

B. IDENTIFY   Provide your personal definition of Positive Influence.

_____

_____

_____

_____

C. UNDERSTAND   Describe the importance of Positive Influence.

_____

_____

BENEFITS:

_____

_____

_____

D. LEARN   Describe how to learn Positive Influence.

_____

_____

_____

_____

E. APPLY AND MODEL   List ways to practice.

_____

_____

_____

_____

LINK

The next chapter covers the Self-Management competency area and discusses four important emotional intelligence skills—Drive Strength, Commitment Ethic, Time Management, and Positive Change. The Drive Strength and Commitment Ethic skills are closely related to the Leadership competency discussion and are essential for high levels of academic and career achievement. Effectively managing your schedule to fulfill your obligations and responsibilities in a timely manner is one of the most visible emotional intelligence skills. The Positive Change skill allows you to be flexible and resilient in a stressful and demanding world, and it is the secret to self-renewal.

Academic and Career Success
Planner Activities

ACTIVITY 4.1	CREATE AN ENVIRONMENT FOR HIGH ACHIEVEMENT

Learning Environment

Your motivation to achieve and your sense of well-being are influenced by how you perceive and engage yourself in the unique learning environment of your college. Indicate how you see and experience your current learning environment by placing an X on one of the seven spaces between each pair of words. Connect the X's to see how you feel about your college learning environment. Total your score and locate it on the profile.

My College's Learning Environment

	1	2	3	4	5	6	7	
HURTFUL								HELPFUL
REJECTING								ACCEPTING
CONFUSING								CLEAR
COLD								WARM
BORING								EXCITING
HOSTILE								FRIENDLY
COMPETITIVE								COOPERATIVE
EASY								CHALLENGING
MEANINGLESS								MEANINGFUL
DANGEROUS								SAFE

Low	Moderate	High

2 4 6 8 10 12 14 16 18 20 22 24 26 28 30 32 34 36 38 40 42 44 46 48 50 52 54 56 58 60 62 64 66 68 70

What actions can you take to feel more comfortable and satisfied in the learning environment?

CHAPTER 5

Self-Management Skills

DRIVE STRENGTH, COMMITMENT ETHIC, TIME MANAGEMENT, AND POSITIVE CHANGE

The Emotional Skills Assessment Process (ESAP) was one of the most meaningful growth activities I have ever experienced in school. It allowed me to view myself more objectively! Sometimes a person can tell you how they see you, but only you can be the best judge of yourself. This course definitely allowed students to get a better understanding of themselves, their career goals, and overall how they can positively shape their lives. It allowed me to better understand how to achieve my goals in college and life!

STUDENT
*South Texas College,
McAllen, Texas*

Preview

This chapter highlights the skills that are central to the behavior of high-achieving, productive students who learn to motivate themselves by setting meaningful personal goals, managing their time and resources, completing assignments, and learning to be flexible in response to unexpected demands and changes. Effective self-management is the key to high levels of academic and career success.

The ensuing discussion's most important message is that accepting responsibility for your own learning and your own success is the first step to improving your achievement. A conscious decision to be the best person that you can be is within the domain of the cognitive mind. The emotional mind provides the energy to achieve your goals and sparks the happiness that results from doing something important to you—and doing it very well.

The Drive Strength skill incorporates energy from the emotional system and requires that you develop the ability to set clear and meaningful personal goals. The ability to motivate yourself, focus energy, and achieve goals is an initial step toward personal excellence. Commitment ethic is the closure skill that many people fail to develop. The emotional outcome of this skill is experienced internally as pride and observed externally as dependability.

The increasing demands and rapid changes characteristic of an Internet-connected world require a level of productivity and personal resilience beyond normal levels. As people respond to the increasing academic and work demands of the twenty-first century, Time Management and Positive Change skills become more essential.

The ability to remain flexible and open to change requires cognitive, emotional, and behavioral skills. The change process presented in this chapter is a systematic approach that integrates the cognitive and experiential systems. The structure and process of change presented is the key to developing resiliency. The ability to confront problems, go through emotions, and change behavior is extremely important to personal well-being and physical health.

DRIVE STRENGTH

Cognitive Focus: Achieving goals that feel good

Emotional Focus: Feeling better through my achievements

Action Focus: Choosing goals that fit my personal values

Definition

Drive Strength is reflected by goal achievement—it is your ability to complete meaningful goals that give you personal satisfaction and positive feelings. Improving your ability to achieve goals involves learning a specific process called *action goal setting* that you can apply and practice on a daily basis. See Exhibit 5.1 for *EI Man's* definition of Drive Strength.

EXHIBIT 5.1   EI SKILL: DRIVE STRENGTH

III. Self-Management Skills
Drive Strength

The Strength to Drive on to your goals comes from within. You need the internal power to make yourself keep going even when things get really tough and all you want to do is "hang it up."

Then, once you do "hang in there," you have the experience to fortify yourself the next time so many obstacles show up: you just keep going.

> DO YOU HAVE THE POWER TO PERSEVERE? IS YOUR INTERNAL ENGINE ABLE TO KEEP UP WITH ALL THE EXTERNAL THINGS THAT WEAR YOU DOWN? CAN YOU KEEP YOUR GOAL IN SIGHT WHEN THINGS GET TO BE "JUST TOO MUCH?" IF THE ANSWERS ARE ALL YES, THEN YOU DO, INDEED, HAVE DRIVE STRENGTH!

EMOTIONAL INTELLIGENCE LESSON 8: DRIVE STRENGTH

STEP A

Self-Assessment: Explore

Read each statement, determine whether the statement applies to you Most Often (M), Sometimes (S), or Least Often (L), and circle the applicable letter–number combination.

1. I set specific goals for my life and career.   M=2 S=1 L=0

2. When working at a task, I evaluate my progress periodically and obtain concrete feedback from my supervisor.   M=2 S=1 L=0

3. When involved in a task, I never think how I will feel if I fail.   M=2 S=1 L=0

4. When working on a committee, I like to see that plans are followed through efficiently.   M=2 S=1 L=0

5. I prefer things to be challenging (involving the risk of failure).   M=2 S=1 L=0

6. At work, I spend most of my time and energy on important projects.   M=2 S=1 L=0

7. I willingly undertake challenging projects that involve the risk of failure.   M=2 S=1 L=0

  8. I set daily goals for myself.   M=2 S=1 L=0

  9. I think more about success than failure when beginning a new task.   M=2 S=1 L=0

 10. Despite the uncertainty of the future, it pays to make plans.   M=2 S=1 L=0

 11. When proceeding with a difficult task, I think of all of the available resources so that I successfully accomplish the task.   M=2 S=1 L=0

 12. I feel my present work is satisfying.   M=2 S=1 L=0

 13. When working on a difficult task, I am aware of and try to improve personal weaknesses that may interfere with the task's successful completion.   M=2 S=1 L=0

 14. I prefer projects that require an intensive effort or long-term commitment.   M=2 S=1 L=0

 15. Planning activities in advance does not take the fun out of life.   M=2 S=1 L=0

 16. I can keep my mind on a task for a long period of time.   M=2 S=1 L=0

 17. I do not give up easily when confronted with a difficult problem.   M=2 S=1 L=0

 18. On work projects, I would rather work with an expert in the field than with a friend or someone I know.   M=2 S=1 L=0

 19. I stick to a job even when I do not feel like it.   M=2 S=1 L=0

 20. I finish things that I start.   M=2 S=1 L=0

 21. I set priorities and meet objectives effectively.   M=2 S=1 L=0

 22. I have more than enough energy to get me through the day.   M=2 S=1 L=0

 23. I am an achiever.   M=2 S=1 L=0

 24. I have a strong desire to be successful in the things that I set out to do.   M=2 S=1 L=0

 25. When I begin a difficult task, I am motivated more by the thought of success than by the thought of failure.   M=2 S=1 L=0

Stop and add your score. *(Max. score = 50)*   **TOTAL SCORE** _____

Transfer your score to the graph in Step B and to the appropriate profile on pages 173–174.

STEP B

Self-Awareness: Identify

Drive Strength is a Self-Management skill that enables you to manage yourself in life and work. To be successful, satisfied, and happy, you must learn to motivate yourself to achieve meaningful goals in life.

10 14 18 22 26	30 34 38	42 44 46 50
DEVELOP	STRENGTHEN	ENHANCE
You can benefit from learning about and understanding the Drive Strength skill. Work through the lesson to fully develop this important Self-Management skill.	You currently identify the Drive Strength skill as one that is at an average level of development. You can improve this skill and make it a strength.	You are claiming the Drive Strength skill as a current strength. Continue to find ways to refine and enhance this important skill.

STEP C

Self-Knowledge: Understand

Setting and accomplishing meaningful personal goals on a daily basis is one of the most important skills for positive mental health and productive living. People experience depression and a general loss of energy when their lives do not contain meaningful behaviors and feelings of accomplishment. Goal achievement is a personal skill that creates positive feelings about yourself and your behavior.

When a person stops doing the things that are personally important (fun, interesting, exciting) and is not feeling good, she says, "I have lost my drive." Drive is not something that you lose or find. *You* create a strong drive by establishing clear goals that are congruent with your important values and beliefs, and then you are supplied with energy from your emotional mind.

The most important aspect of action goal setting is defining your own values and beliefs—what is important to you as a person. Your goals must fit your values so that the accomplishments lead to positive feelings. We have all learned to set goals that involve what we should do. When we spend all our energy doing only what we should or must do, we usually end up feeling tired, sad, and empty. Action goal setting (meaningful activity) is a sure way to change boredom and depression, and it is a way to keep ourselves happy and feeling good.

When a person establishes a meaningful personal goal, he is being active, not reactive. This is one of the keys to positive mental health. For example, if you wait to have a good day, the wait is sometimes a long one. Goal setting is a process that ensures that good things will happen on a particular day because you accept responsibility for setting and accomplishing the behaviors that let you feel good that day.

Action goal setting helps a person learn that she can direct and focus energy to accomplish behaviors that are satisfying. This process builds feelings of self-control and reminds you that you can exercise choice in your behaviors. When you want to feel better, happier, or healthier as a person, you must start doing more things that you really like and value. Each meaningful goal that you set and accomplish builds your self-esteem and self-confidence.

STEP D

Self-Development: Learn

To select a goal that you want to accomplish, to feel good about, you must first determine what you value. Ask yourself what you value most. What is most important to you? Honesty? Success? Independence? Relationships with others? Being a better friend? Freedom? Achievement? Kindness? Loyalty?

In the space provided, describe an important goal that you believe you can achieve. The goal you select should fit your most important personal values.

Goal statement. The most important goal that I can accomplish to feel better is:

_____

_____

_____

_____

_____

STEP E

Self-Improvement: Apply and Model

As you begin to practice action goal setting, use the following checklist as a guide for each goal you set.

GOAL CHECKLIST

Use the goal statement that you prepared in Step D and complete the checklist.

Yes   No

☐   ☐   Does the goal fit my personal values and belief system? Will it let me feel better when I accomplish it?

☐   ☐   Is the goal important to me? Do I really want to do it?

☐ ☐   Is the goal specific and presented without an alternative? Does it describe a behavior well enough so that I know exactly what to do?

☐ ☐   Is the goal tangible? Can I visualize the goal?

☐ ☐   Is the goal achievable? Am I capable of doing the goal behavior?

☐ ☐   Is the goal measurable by some criteria?

☐ ☐   Have I set a specific target date to complete the goal?

EXERCISE

Complete the following exercise and use it as you develop the Drive Strength emotional skill into an intentional habit.

A. EXPLORE   How do you think, feel, and behave when you use this skill?

_____

_____

_____

Cognitive Focus: Achieving goals that feel good

_____

_____

_____

Emotional Focus: Feeling better through my achievements

_____

_____

_____

Action Focus: Choosing goals that fit my personal values

_____

_____

_____

B. IDENTIFY   Provide your personal definition of Drive Strength.

_____

_____

_____

C. UNDERSTAND   Describe the importance of Drive Strength.

BENEFITS:

D. LEARN   Describe how to learn Drive Strength.

E. APPLY AND MODEL   List ways to practice.

COMMITMENT ETHIC

Cognitive Focus: Finishing what I start
Emotional Focus: Feeling good about getting things done
Action Focus: Choosing behaviors true to my personal standards and values

Definition

Commitment Ethic is an emotional skill reflected by the ability to complete tasks, assignments, and responsibilities dependably and successfully. People with a high level of Commitment Ethic skill are inner-directed, self-motivated, and persistent when completing projects, regardless of the difficulties involved. Commitment Ethic is a dedication to task completion that produces excitement and pride, not fatigue and sacrifice. *EI Man's* thoughts about Commitment Ethic are outlined in Exhibit 5.2.

EXHIBIT 5.2	EI SKILL: COMMITMENT ETHIC

Commitment Ethic

A commitment is a pledge you make to yourself or others that you will engage and stay engaged in what is necessary and right. When you make a commitment, you are saying that this is not just a "one-time deal." Rather it is something that will continue to be done as long as it is necessary to do so. When you make an ethic out of being committed, you make it into a rule of life; one that you do not stray from, no matter what should arise.

> TO BE COMMITTED IS TO MAKE SINCERE PROMISES TO YOURSELF AND OTHERS
> THAT YOU WILL DO WHAT YOU SAY YOU WILL DO.
> A MAN OR WOMAN IS ONLY AS GOOD AS THEIR WORD.

EMOTIONAL INTELLIGENCE LESSON 9: COMMITMENT ETHIC

STEP A

Self-Assessment: Explore

Read each statement, determine whether the statement applies to you Most Often (M), Sometimes (S), or Least Often (L), and circle the applicable letter–number combination.

1. I am considered a dependable person.   M=2 S=1 L=0
2. When something has to be done, people turn to me.   M=2 S=1 L=0
3. I have often worked day and night on projects to meet a deadline that I have agreed to or set for myself.   M=2 S=1 L=0
4. I have a strong sense of right and wrong for myself, and I behave accordingly.   M=2 S=1 L=0
5. I have a solid feeling of confidence in my ability to create a good life for myself.   M=2 S=1 L=0
6. When I decide to do something, I carry through and do it.   M=2 S=1 L=0
7. I do not procrastinate.   M=2 S=1 L=0
8. In almost any area that I try, I really do well.   M=2 S=1 L=0
9. I am a "hard worker," even when I am not supervised.   M=2 S=1 L=0
10. People admire my ability to accomplish what I set out to do.   M=2 S=1 L=0

11. Even when I encounter personal difficulties, I complete assignments and obligations.   M=2 S=1 L=0

12. I rarely fail at anything that I consider important.   M=2 S=1 L=0

Stop and add your score. *(Max. score = 24)*   **TOTAL SCORE** _____

Transfer your score to the graph in Step B and to the appropriate profile on pages 173–174.

Transfer your score to the graph in Step B and to the appropriate profile on pages 173–174.

STEP B

Self-Awareness: Identify

Commitment Ethic is a Self-Management skill that enables you to manage yourself in life and work. To be successful, satisfied, and happy, you must learn to make commitments and complete projects in a dependable manner.

8 10 12 14	16 18 20	22 24
DEVELOP	STRENGTHEN	ENHANCE
You can benefit from learning about and understanding the Commitment Ethic skill. Work through the lesson to fully develop this important Self-Management skill.	You currently identify the Commitment Ethic skill as one that is at an average level of development. You can improve this skill and make it a strength.	You are claiming the Commitment Ethic skill as a current strength. Continue to find ways to refine and enhance this important skill.

STEP C

Self-Knowledge: Understand

The Commitment Ethic skill has an internal cognitive component (a promise to yourself) and an observable behavioral component (consistent completion of accepted responsibilities). People often accept responsibility for things they do not really want to do or care about; punish themselves for being a failure, bored, and unmotivated; and *feel* guilty about not having done what they did not want to do in the first place. A good way to understand the skill's importance is *trying* to make yourself do something that you do not really *want* to do. Trying is the tyrant "should" of the cognitive mind, and "want" is the energetic and playful companion of the emotional mind. If you are true to yourself and set meaningful personal goals, your ability to commit will emerge and push you toward completing the goal so that you can enjoy feeling happy and proud of your accomplishment.

Commitment Ethic is the inseparable companion of high achievement and personal excellence and is an extremely important predictor of personal achievement and satisfaction. It arises from a core value held by a person who becomes the best he can become and commits to excellence in all phases of life and work. The skill is observable as dependability and persistence—the person on whom you can count to do what she says and do it extremely well.

STEP D

Self-Development: Learn

Commitment Ethic is an inward promise to do what you say, finish what you start, and be proud of what you produce. It is fueled by purpose and emotion. To strengthen your Commitment Ethic, you have to establish, accept, and dedicate your energy and effort to completing meaningful goals.

You have the potential within you to do many things very well. The key to improving this skill is to focus and direct your energy and effort toward completing goals that increase your self-esteem and create a feeling of pride when they are accomplished.

Value clarification and decision making are prerequisite skills for increasing your Commitment Ethic. Directing energy and effort toward goals that you do not value leaves you empty of feelings and fatigued. We can all complete tasks that we do not care about or value. The feeling produced by completing these "should do" or "must do" goals is more often relief than pride.

STEP E

Self-Improvement: Apply and Model

As a way of increasing and strengthening your Commitment Ethic, inventory your most important achievements of the past. Everyone has this positive history—memories of times and events when we felt proud, special, and positive. List three positive achievements (events) from your past that produced feelings of pride and self-appreciation, and then describe any important values represented by each achievement.

Positive achievements:

1. _____

2. _____

3. _____

Important values represented by my achievements:

1. _____

2. _____

3. _____

Using this information from your past, set three new goals. These goals should be ones that will produce results that bring you positive feelings and a sense of pride.

1. _____

2. _____

3. _____

Commit yourself to completing these goals by a specific date as a way to experience the rewards of an increased Commitment Ethic. Check for hesitations. Do not commit to goals that you do not value. Decide which goal has the highest priority for you now. Complete that one first, and enjoy the benefits of your energy.

> It is a mistake to speak of dedication as a sacrifice. Every man knows that there is exhilaration in intense effort applied toward a meaningful end.
>
> JOHN GARDNER

EXERCISE

Complete the following exercise and use it as you develop the Commitment Ethic emotional skill into an intentional habit.

A. EXPLORE   How do you think, feel, and behave when you use this skill?

_____

_____

_____

Cognitive Focus: Finishing what I start

_____

_____

_____

Emotional Focus: Feeling good about getting things done

_____

_____

_____

Action Focus: Choosing behaviors true to my personal standards and values

_____

B. IDENTIFY   Provide your personal definition of Commitment Ethic.

C. UNDERSTAND   Describe the importance of Commitment Ethic.

BENEFITS:

D. LEARN   Describe how to learn Commitment Ethic.

E. APPLY AND MODEL   List ways to practice.

TIME MANAGEMENT

Cognitive Focus: Getting important things done

Emotional Focus: Feeling better about how I use time

Action Focus: Choosing better ways to manage myself

EXHIBIT 5.3	EI SKILL: TIME MANAGEMENT

Time Management

An effective Time Manager knows that time just keeps flowing, so go with the flow.
  Prioritize what you need to do: first things first.
  Schedule yourself by the time you have: Use your time wisely by making your tasks and your leisure fit together in a well-scheduled day, week or semester. Don't put off to tomorrow what could easily be done today. Procrastination is your greatest enemy.

> TIME MARCHES ON, YOU CAN'T CONTROL TIME, BUT YOU CAN CONTROL YOURSELF IN RELATION TO TIME. TREAT TIME AS YOUR FRIEND, NOT YOUR ENEMY. IF YOU KNOW HOW TO USE YOUR TIME WISELY AND EFFICIENTLY, YOU WILL ALWAYS HAVE ENOUGH TIME TO DO WHAT YOU NEED TO DO.

Definition

Time Management is the ability to organize tasks into a personally productive time schedule and use time effectively to complete the tasks. Effective Time Management is the ability to *actively manage* time instead of *responding* to the demands of time. *EI Man* advises us to treat time as our friend. See Exhibit 5.3 Time Management.

EMOTIONAL INTELLIGENCE LESSON 10: TIME MANAGEMENT

STEP A

Self-Assessment: Explore

Read each statement, determine whether the statement applies to you Most Often (M), Sometimes (S), or Least Often (L), and circle the applicable letter–number combination.

1. I organize my responsibilities into an efficient personal time schedule. M=2 S=1 L=0
2. I set objectives for myself and then successfully complete them within a specific time period. M=2 S=1 L=0
3. I plan and complete my work schedule. M=2 S=1 L=0
4. If I were being evaluated on job effectiveness, I would receive high ratings in managing my workday. M=2 S=1 L=0

5. I waste very little time.   M=2 S=1 L=0

6. I know exactly how much time I need to complete projects   M=2 S=1 L=0
   and assignments.

7. I am an efficient and well-organized person.   M=2 S=1 L=0

8. I effectively manage my time and do not procrastinate.   M=2 S=1 L=0

9. I am among the first to arrive at meetings or events.   M=2 S=1 L=0

10. I am on time for my appointments.   M=2 S=1 L=0

11. I am able to work effectively on several projects at the same time   M=2 S=1 L=0
    with good results.

12. I control my responsibilities instead of being controlled by them.   M=2 S=1 L=0

Stop and add your score. *(Max. score = 24)*   **TOTAL SCORE** _____

Transfer your score to the graph in Step B and to the appropriate profile on pages 173–174.

STEP B

Self-Awareness: Identify

Time Management is a Self-Management skill that enables you to manage yourself in life and work. To be successful, satisfied, and happy, you must learn to view time as a valuable resource and use time effectively.

5 8 10 12	14 16 18	20 22 24
DEVELOP	STRENGTHEN	ENHANCE
You can benefit from learning about and understanding the Time Management skill. Work through the lesson to fully develop this important Self-Management skill.	You currently identify the Time Management skill as one that is at an average level of development. You can improve this skill and make it a strength.	You are claiming the Time Management skill as a current strength. Continue to find ways to refine and enhance this important skill.

STEP C

Self-Knowledge: Understand

Positive mental health and productive living require that we actively manage our responsibilities within time restrictions. An important by-product of good Time Management is a feeling of self-control—we are managing our responsibilities, not being managed by them. In essence, effective Time Management is self-managed and self-directed behavior that allows us to accomplish daily tasks with less effort and emotional intensity.

Your goal in developing effective Time Management skills is to achieve self-direction in your behavior that leads to balance and harmony in your thoughts, feelings, and behaviors. When your behavior is self-directed, you experience a feeling of self-control and mastery when responding to the demands of daily living.

Our research and experience in academic and corporate settings has shown that the behaviors related to effective Time Management are absolutely essential to success and personal well-being. Productivity, the completion of assigned tasks and accepted responsibilities, and the achievement of meaningful personal goals are directly related to your ability to complete tasks within a specified time frame. The Time Management behaviors that you will explore now are "musts" for academic and career success. If your cognitive mind represents them as "shoulds," your emotional mind will let you know what it would like to do instead. Use self-assertion to remind yourself that you are willing to accept the responsibility for doing the task because you want to be successful.

Remember that effective time management is self-managed and self-directed behavior that allows you to accomplish daily tasks efficiently and with minimum stress. Nothing stirs up the emotional mind more than trying to make yourself do something that you really do not want to do. This struggle is usually described by the word *procrastination.* Procrastination is the "dark side" of effective Time Management. Most of us have heard our internal voice whisper such things as "Let's play now, and work later" or "I do not feel like doing that now; there will be time tomorrow." By now, your increased level of self-awareness lets you know that the emotional mind always prefers pleasure to pain.

Personal well-being (happiness, peace of mind, and self-confidence) requires that you actively manage and complete your responsibilities with good results. This is especially important when you face a task or assignment that you do not want to do. If you wait for the emotional mind to signal its approval to start, you are in for a long and conflicted struggle. Effective Time Management has a cognitive component that tells us that action in the present is a better choice than setting up an internal battle of the "should" and the "want" and ending up disappointed and angry about poor performance. "Just do it" is a good self-statement in this situation. Be sure to let your emotional mind know that as soon as you finish this unpleasant task the two of you will have some real fun to celebrate the victory.

STEP D

Self-Development: Learn

Effective Time Management means more control and balance in your life, more spontaneity, flexibility, and freedom in living. Increased self-control and effective Time Management begins with planning. Planning involves bringing the future into the present and deciding what you are willing to do about it now. When planning, you must decide what the important objectives are in your life and then establish priorities every day in relation to these objectives. Most of what we do on a daily basis is done by habit. Your attitude toward things you do and the time you take to do them is a consistent pattern of thoughts or a habit. Your thoughts influence your feelings and your feelings influence your behaviors.

The first step in learning effective Time Management is to examine your thoughts about time and its value. Think about Time Management as self-management. You can learn how to better manage yourself so that you can do more things that you want to do and spend less time struggling over what you have to do. How you choose to spend time can lead to good feelings and accomplishment or fatigue and boredom.

Time is highly personal, and we all get the same amount each day. Each of us uses these hours the way we want, and how we choose to spend our time determines the quality of our lives. As you plan your time on a daily basis, you should list your goals and prioritize them by deciding which goals are most important. When you accomplish personally meaningful goals, you experience positive feelings. You can improve the quality of your life one day at a time by achieving goals that allow you to feel that your time has been used effectively.

STEP E

Self-Improvement: Apply and Model

Set aside 15 minutes (early morning or evening). List 10 important personal goals that you want to accomplish during the next few months. Focus on personally meaningful goals that you can accomplish in about 2 weeks.

1. _____

2. _____

3. _____

4. _____

5. _____

6. _____

7. _____

8. _____

9. _____

10. _____

Now, prioritize the goals by placing an **A** by the most important, a **B** by those second in importance, and a **C** by those that are the least important.

GOAL CHECKLIST

Choose one of the goals that you labeled with an **A** from the list you made in Step E and complete the checklist.

Yes No

☐ ☐ Does the goal fit my personal values and belief system? Will it let me feel better when I accomplish it?

☐ ☐ Is the goal important to me? Do I really want to do it?

☐ ☐ Is the goal specific and presented without an alternative? Does it describe a behavior well enough so that I know exactly what to do?

☐ ☐ Is the goal tangible? Can I visualize the goal?

☐ ☐ Is the goal achievable? Am I capable of doing the goal behavior?

☐ ☐ Is the goal measurable by some criteria?

☐ ☐ Have I set a specific target date to complete the goal?

After you have used the checklist for your chosen goal, complete the process with the remaining nine goals. Are your goals realistic? Can each goal be completed within the next 2 weeks? If your answers to these questions are "yes," you are ready to begin the necessary work to achieve the goals.

EXERCISE

Complete the following exercise and use it as you develop the Time Management emotional skill into an intentional habit.

A. EXPLORE   How do you think, feel, and behave when you use this skill?

_____

_____

_____

_____

Cognitive Focus: Getting important things done

_____

_____

_____

Emotional Focus: Feeling better about how I use time

_____

_____

_____

_____

Action Focus: Choosing better ways to manage myself

_____

_____

_____

B. IDENTIFY   Provide your personal definition of Time Management.

_____

_____

_____

_____

_____

C. UNDERSTAND   Describe the importance of Time Management.

_____

BENEFITS:

_____

_____

_____

D. LEARN   Describe how to learn Time Management.

_____

_____

_____
_____
_____

E. APPLY AND MODEL   List ways to practice.

_____
_____
_____
_____

POTENTIAL PROBLEM AREA: CHANGE ORIENTATION

Change Orientation is a reflection of your level of satisfaction with your current behavior. Your view of how satisfied you are is an important starting point for planning personal change. Positive Change is essential to developing and maintaining mental and physical health. Applying the Emotional Learning System gives you a practical structure for completing a personal change. Each time you pause, assess, and become aware of the need for change, you are able to improve your behavior.

POSITIVE CHANGE

Cognitive Focus: Understanding personal change

Emotional Focus: Feeling good about making personal changes

Action Focus: Choosing healthy ways to make personal changes

Definition

Change Orientation is the degree to which an individual is or is not satisfied with current behavior and the magnitude of change necessary or desired to develop personal and professional effectiveness. It includes the degree to which a person is motivated and ready for change. Change Orientation must be understood and converted to the _Positive Change_ emotional skill to achieve excellence in all areas of life. Review Exhibit 5.4, Change Orientation, and see if you agree with _EI Man's_ thoughts about change.

EXHIBIT 5.4	CHANGE ORIENTATION

Change Orientation

When something brand new happens in your life, can you "go with the flow" and make a positive change that will satisfy yourself in the new situation? When you are dissatisfied with yourself, can you make a change that makes you a happier person? If you said yes, then you have a handle on Positive Personal Change. If not, you would benefit greatly by learning this very necessary skill.

> NOT EVERY CHANGE IS NECESSARY, THAT'S FOR YOU TO DECIDE. DO YOU RESIST CHANGE MERELY BECAUSE IT'S NEW? OR DO YOU THINK IT THROUGH TO SEE IF A CHANGE MIGHT HELP YOU? DECIDING TO MAKE NECESSARY CHANGES ARE SOME OF THE MOST IMPORTANT DECISIONS YOU CAN MAKE.

EMOTIONAL INTELLIGENCE LESSON 11: POSITIVE CHANGE

STEP A

Self-Assessment: Explore

Read each statement, determine whether the statement applies to you Most Often (M), Sometimes (S), or Least Often (L), and circle the applicable letter–number combination.

1. One of the things that I must change is how I feel about myself as a person.   M=2 S=1 L=0

2. One of the things that I must change is the way that I relate to my family.   M=2 S=1 L=0

3. I am not satisfied with the way I manage my time.   M=2 S=1 L=0

4. I should change my job (career).   M=2 S=1 L=0

5. I must change the way I handle stress and tension.   M=2 S=1 L=0

6. I am not satisfied with my ability to handle problems or conflicts.   M=2 S=1 L=0

7. I am not satisfied with the amount of energy I expend being successful in life.   M=2 S=1 L=0

8. I am not satisfied with my leadership ability.   M=2 S=1 L=0

9. I am not satisfied with my decision-making ability.   M=2 S=1 L=0

10. One of the things that I must change is the way I relate to people.   M=2 S=1 L=0
11. I am not satisfied with the way I handle intimate relationships.   M=2 S=1 L=0
12. One of the things that I must change is how I take care of my body.   M=2 S=1 L=0

Stop and add your score. (*Max. score = 24*)   **TOTAL SCORE** _____

Transfer your score to the graph in Step B and to the appropriate profile on pages 173–174.

STEP B

Self-Awareness: Identify

Change Orientation is a reflection of a satisfaction or a dissatisfaction with current emotional skills and abilities. Change Orientation must be understood and converted to the powerful emotional skill of Positive Change.

1 3 5 7	9 11 13	16 18 21 24
LOW	NORMAL	HIGH
A low score on Change Orientation is positive. This means that you are claiming Positive Change as a current strength. Continue to find ways to refine and enhance the Positive Change skill.	You currently identify the Positive Change skill as one that is at an average level of development. You can improve this skill and make it a strength.	A high score on Change Orientation indicates a potential problem area and a recognition of the need to change. You can benefit from learning and improving the Positive Change skill. Work through the lesson to fully develop the important self-management skill of Positive Change.

STEP C

Self-Knowledge: Understand

Your feeling of competence (self-confidence) improves as you develop specific skills to positively self-manage difficult situations. You feel better about your ability to handle difficult personal, academic, and career demands (stressors). To improve your competence in handling personally challenging stressors, it is helpful to have a systematic approach to follow to change your behavior. When you identify a behavior that you want to change, use the Positive Change Process described in Exhibit 5.5 as a guide to understand and clarify how to make the behavioral change that you desire.

EXHIBIT 5.5	THE POSITIVE CHANGE PROCESS

Steps	Change Process
STEP 1	Identify (target) a specific behavior for change.
STEP 2	Initiate an internal dialogue to check your conscious willingness to change. Is this an area I want to change to feel more comfortable? Am I willing to change?
STEP 3	State the desired change specifically and in line with your personal values: What I specifically want to change is how I _____.
STEP 4	Identify the internal (within yourself) or external event (stressor) that seems to elicit (cause) the behavior you want to change.
STEP 5	Identify your thoughts, attitudes, or beliefs in relation to the stressor (cognitive component).
STEP 6	Describe, clarify, and assess your emotional reaction to the stressor (emotional component).
STEP 7	Identify, dispute, and challenge self-defeating and irrational beliefs; check catastrophic thinking and critical self-talk.
STEP 8	Use your personal resources to create rational beliefs and substitute these for the irrational beliefs identified in Step 7. Develop and practice personally helpful self-statements. Use the Emotional Learning System to develop constructive and critical thinking.
STEP 9	Implement and practice the process of cognitive restructuring when dealing with personal stressors in your daily living. Focus on the task and set a specific behavioral goal to handle the problem (behavioral component).
STEP 10	Select a specific skill training experience to reinforce and facilitate the new behavior (e.g., stress management).

STEP D

Self-Development: Learn

Remember that self-efficacy (self-confidence) is situation specific and that positive gains in one area contribute to an increase in self-esteem. If you target a specific behavior for change (e.g., decreasing test anxiety) and actually improve your performance on tests, the positive behavioral change contributes to better feelings about yourself (improved self-esteem). You experience increased self-confidence because you have learned to exercise control over your anxiety level—the situation is now positive and productive, not excessively stressful and self-defeating.

STEP E

Self-Improvement: Apply and Model

On a separate piece of paper, describe three behaviors that you feel you should change. Then, for each identified behavior, follow the steps outlined in Exhibit 5.5. Discuss the results with your classmates.

EXERCISE

Complete the following exercise and use it as you develop the Positive Change emotional skill into an intentional habit.

A. EXPLORE   How do you think, feel, and behave when you use this skill?

_____

_____

_____

Cognitive Focus: Understanding personal change

_____

_____

_____

Emotional Focus: Feeling good about making personal changes

_____

_____

_____

Action Focus: Choosing healthy ways to make personal changes

_____

_____

_____

B. IDENTIFY   Provide your personal definition of Positive Change.

_____

_____

_____

_____

_____

C. UNDERSTAND   Describe the importance of Positive Change.

_____

BENEFITS:

_____

_____

D. LEARN   Describe how to learn Positive Change.

_____

_____

_____

_____

E. APPLY AND MODEL   List ways to practice.

_____

_____

_____

_____

_____

LINK

The next chapter presents the Intrapersonal competency area and its Self-Esteem and Stress Management emotional intelligence skills. It presents a view of Self-Esteem that is optimistic and dynamic. Remind yourself of your value as a person, and learn how to manage stress to keep yourself emotionally secure and healthy.

Academic and Career Success Planner Activities

ACTIVITY 5.1	GOALS CALENDAR FOR HIGH PERSONAL ACHIEVEMENT

Month_____ Year_____

EI Skills Focus:

Goal Achievement

Motivating yourself and directing energy to achieve meaningful personal goals.
The ability to focus on goal-directed behaviors leading to high achievement.

S	M	T	W	T	F	S
○	○	○	○	○	○	○
○	○	○	○	○	○	○
○	○	○	○	○	○	○
○	○	○	○	○	○	○
○	○	○	○	○	○	○
○	○	○	○	○	○	○

Will Do Behaviors: Goal Achievement

Priority	When	Target Date
1._____	1._____	1._____
2._____	2._____	2._____
3._____	3._____	3._____
How important?	How urgent?	Completion Date

Goal Achievement Map

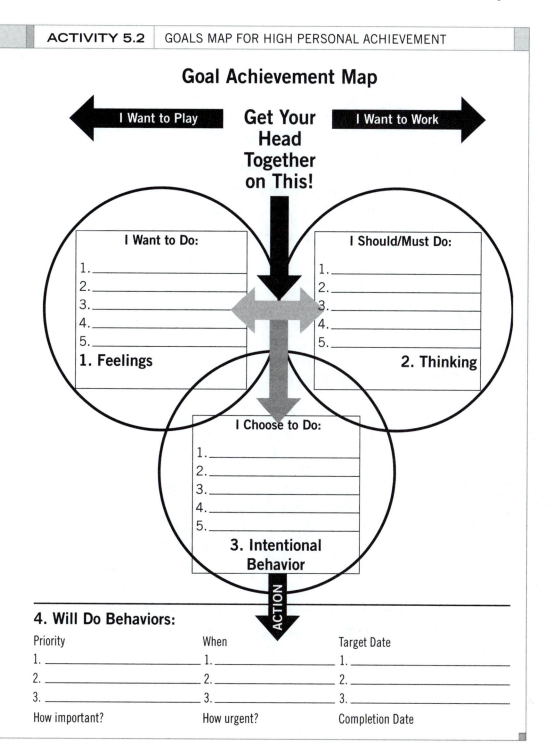

I Want to Play

Get Your Head Together on This!

I Want to Work

I Want to Do:

1. _____
2. _____
3. _____
4. _____
5. _____

1. Feelings

I Should/Must Do:

1. _____
2. _____
3. _____
4. _____
5. _____

2. Thinking

I Choose to Do:

1. _____
2. _____
3. _____
4. _____
5. _____

3. Intentional Behavior

ACTION

4. Will Do Behaviors:

Priority	When	Target Date
1. _____	1. _____	1. _____
2. _____	2. _____	2. _____
3. _____	3. _____	3. _____
How important?	How urgent?	Completion Date

ACTIVITY 5.3	COMMITMENT ETHIC CALENDAR FOR HIGH PERSONAL ACHIEVEMENT

Month_____ Year_____

El Skills Focus:

Commitment Ethic

Being persistent and resilient in the face of challenging problems.
Finishing what you start with good results.

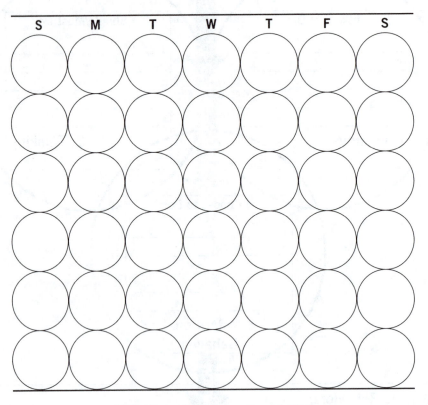

| S | M | T | W | T | F | S |

Will Do Behaviors: Commitment Ethic

Priority	When	Target Date
1._____	1._____	1._____
2._____	2._____	2._____
3._____	3._____	3._____
How important?	How urgent?	Completion Date

ACTIVITY 5.4	CLARIFY YOUR COMMITMENT ETHIC AND INCREASE YOUR PERSONAL RESPONSIBILITY FOR ACHIEVING YOUR GOALS

Commitment Ethic

Being dependable and consistent in personal goal achievement.

Key: Set goals that are clear, specific, and consistent with your important needs and values. Before setting and starting a personal goal, **ask:**

- Does the goal fit my needs, values, beliefs?
- Is the goal important and meaningful to me?
- Do I want to do it?
- Is the goal specific (written down/visualized)?
- Is the goal achievable?
- Have I set a target date for completion?
- Will the goal hurt me or others?

PERSONAL RESPONSIBILITY
Finishing What You Start with Good Results and Positive Feelings

EI SKILLS
- Time Management
- Goal Achievement
- Commitment Ethic
- Assertion
- Stress Management

VALUES/ BELIEFS
- Achievement
- Autonomy
- Equality
- Honesty
- Integrity
- Justice
- Fairness
- Interdependence
- Family
- Independence

CAMPUS RESOURCES
- Mentors
- Professors
- Tutors
- Study Skill Labs
- Computer Skills
- Reading Skills
- Writing Skills
- Speaking Skills
- Career Counseling

NEEDS
- Good Relationships
- Positive Self-View
- Respect
- Acceptance
- Belonging
- Safety
- Pleasure
- Pain Avoidance
- Survival

FEELINGS	**THOUGHTS**	**ACTIONS**
EMOTIONAL	**COGNITIVE**	**BEHAVIORAL**

ACTIVITY 5.5	TIME MANAGEMENT CALENDAR FOR HIGH PERSONAL ACHIEVEMENT

Month_____ Year_____

El Skills Focus:

Time Management

Planning and effectively managing yourself by using the resources of time to complete academic requirements and personal goals.

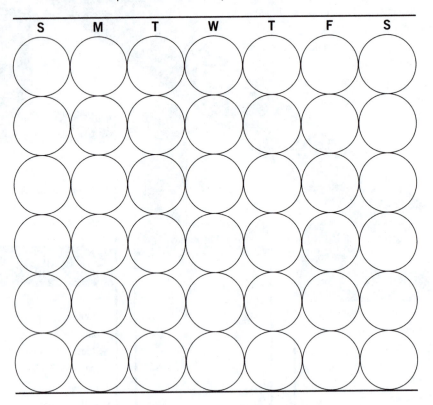

S	M	T	W	T	F	S

Will Do Behaviors: Time Management

Priority	When	Target Date
1._____	1._____	1._____
2._____	2._____	2._____
3._____	3._____	3._____
How important?	How urgent?	Completion Date

ACTIVITY 5.6	TIME TRACKER

Directions:

Using the Time Tracker Chart and coded activities below, start at 12:00 a.m. (midnight) on any day of the week and then record how you spend your time for one whole week. Fill in the days and dates, as appropriate, in the day/date boxes at the top of the chart.

Use the below mentioned keys to record activities that occur within the 168 1-hour blocks available during your week. If you engage in activities that are not listed, then add them to the list. You do not need to use all the categories. Use only those that pertain to you. But make sure you account for all 168 hours!

Keep it simple. Refrain from recording more than three activities during any 1-hour period. Recording more than three activities will make computing your totals for each activity more complicated and difficult than it really needs to be. At the end of the week, compute the total amount of time you spent doing each activity. Then compute how you spent your time in terms of a percentage of the week. Make a pie chart that reflects how you used your time. Are there any surprises? What insights have you learned? Move to Exercise 5.7 and use the Time Watch to gain additional personal clarity about your time.

CODE	YOUR ACTIVITIES
1	Sports or other required activities related to fulfilling scholarship obligations.
2	Caring for a family member
3	Church/spiritual
4	Class time—record actual time spent in the classroom and labs
5	Communicating (telephone, texting, e-mailing, etc.)
6	Commuting (school/work)
7	Finances—paying bills, banking, etc.
8	Groceries/errands
9	House/yard/apartment maintenance
10	Hygiene activities—bathing, shaving, applying makeup, etc.
11	Leadership activities (organizing events, community service, etc.)
12	Partying
13	Physical fitness
14	Preparing meals/eating—breakfast, lunch, dinner, or just snacking, etc.
15	Reading for pleasure
16	Recreation time
17	Relationships (friends, family, significant others)
18	Schoolwork, studying, reading, homework—dorm, home, library
19	Sleeping
20	Surfing the internet and chat rooms
21	Watching TV
22	Working (for income)

TIME TRACKER CHART (A.M.)

Name: _____

Daily activity log: record activities in each hour. *Be accurate!*

	12 A.M. 1 A.M.	1 A.M. 2 A.M.	2 A.M. 3 A.M.	3 A.M. 4 A.M.	4 A.M. 5 A.M.	5 A.M. 6 A.M.	6 A.M. 7 A.M.	7 A.M. 8 A.M.	8 A.M. 9 A.M.	9 A.M. 10 A.M.	10 A.M. 11 A.M.	11 A.M. 12 P.M.
DAY: DATE:												
DAY: DATE:												
DAY: DATE:												
DAY: DATE:												
DAY: DATE:												
DAY: DATE:												
DAY: DATE:												

TIME TRACKER CHART (P.M.)

Name: _____

Daily activity log: record activities in each hour. *Be accurate!*

	12 P.M. 1 P.M.	1 P.M. 2 P.M.	2 P.M. 3 P.M.	3 P.M. 4 P.M.	4 P.M. 5 P.M.	5 P.M. 6 P.M.	6 P.M. 7 P.M.	7 P.M. 8 P.M.	8 P.M. 9 P.M.	9 P.M. 10 P.M.	10 P.M. 11 P.M.	11 P.M. 12 A.M.
DAY: DATE:												
DAY: DATE:												
DAY: DATE:												
DAY: DATE:												
DAY: DATE:												
DAY: DATE:												
DAY: DATE:												

ACTIVITY 5.7	WHAT ARE THE MOST PERSONALLY MEANINGFUL WAYS FOR USING THE TIME YOU HAVE?

Time Watch

Day_____   Time_____

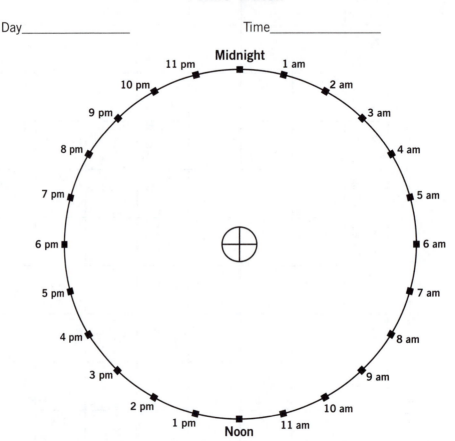

_____   _____   _____

Priority Goals

- **Time Management is the most important academic success skill.**
- **Create days that are meaningful, fun and productive by planning study, work, and play**
- **Pick out one of your busy days.**
- **Complete the Time Watch to see how you use your time.**

STEP1: Show when and how long you use your time for the activities that follow. You have 24 hours in your day. When and for how long do you: Sleep? Eat? Attend class? Work? Study? Play? Relax? Commute/Travel to class? Watch TV? Play video games? Listen to music? Visit with friends? Attend meetings? Surf the Internet?

STEP2: Start with the activities that you do every day such as sleep. Draw a line from the hour that you go to sleep to the center and a line from the hour that you awake. Shade in and label this area as sleep time. Do the same for eating, working, studying, playing, etc. What behaviors do you need to increase or decrease to make the day better for you? Set a priority goal to make the day more meaningful, comfortable, and productive.

CHAPTER 6

Intrapersonal Skills

SELF-ESTEEM AND STRESS MANAGEMENT

First, I shared the information about emotional intelligence with my daughter. Later, we went through the book together!

STUDENT–PARENT
Galveston College,
Galveston, Texas

Preview

Constructive thinking allows you to be imperfect (as all humans are), make mistakes, and remain positive in your evaluation of Self. None of us wants to fail or make serious mistakes, but the risk of failure is always a part of high achievement. What we say to ourselves (self-talk), how we explain our behavior, and what we do to improve our behavior all have a significant impact. This chapter introduces the Intrapersonal competency area and discusses its two emotional intelligence skills—Self-Esteem and Stress Management.

The primary focus of this chapter is to heighten your awareness about your value and worth as a person. Your level of self-esteem is a reflection of your current assessment of how you are doing in the world. Remind yourself that you can change and improve any thought, feeling, or behavior that becomes problematic or self-defeating. This hopefulness and optimism about your ability to change and improve is basic to positive self-esteem.

The attitudinal components of optimism—positive self-worth and self-confidence—are closely related to the effective management of high levels of stress. You must positively value Self to see the value in learning alternatives to self-defeating and self-destructive behaviors. Many high-achieving and competent people damage their emotional and physical health by choosing not to learn and practice stress-management strategies.

Intense levels of emotion and self-defeating behaviors can damage your mental, as well as physical, health. Positive stress management requires a number of inter-related emotional skills. Stress is unavoidable and has many sources. Identifying personal stressors, learning to change self-defeating thoughts, and practicing daily relaxation techniques are the three primary stress-management strategies discussed. Take the time to learn and practice a stress-management strategy daily—not because you have to or should, but simply because you are valuable and want to live a long and healthy life.

SELF-ESTEEM

Cognitive Focus: Learning to value myself more
Emotional Focus: Learning to feel better about myself
Action Focus: Learning to behave in ways that I respect and value

Definition

Self-Esteem is the ability to view Self as positive, competent, and successful. Positive Self-Esteem is the foundation for achievement and a general sense of well-being. It is developed and maintained when one experiences success after effectively dealing with Self, others, and the demands of life. Look at Exhibit 6.1 to learn about some of *El Man's* insights regarding Self-Esteem.

EXHIBIT 6.1	EI SKILL: SELF-ESTEEM

SELF-ESTEEM

Self-esteem is how you feel about yourself. If you see yourself as competent and pretty much always successful, this is how you are going to be: self-confident and able to do what you need to do very well. If you feel bad about yourself because you don't think you have what it takes, then you won't do very well. But self-esteem is not being conceited or arrogant; self-esteem is looking at yourself honestly and liking what you see.

SELF-ESTEEM CAN ALSO BE SEEING YOUR POSITIVE QUALITIES REFLECTED IN OTHER PEOPLE WHOM YOU ADMIRE. LIKE ATTRACTS LIKE AND YOU MAY FIND THE COMPANY OF OTHER PEOPLE WITH HIGH SELF-ESTEEM BENEFICIAL TO YOU.

EMOTIONAL INTELLIGENCE LESSON 12: SELF-ESTEEM

STEP A

Self-Assessment: Explore

Read each statement, determine whether the statement applies to you Most Often (M), Sometimes (S), or Least Often (L), and circle the applicable letter–number combination.

1. I am a cheerful person.   M=2 S=1 L=0
2. I am satisfied with my family relationships.   M=2 S=1 L=0
3. My daily life is full of things that keep me interested.   M=2 S=1 L=0
4. I am an important person.   M=2 S=1 L=0
5. My feelings are not easily hurt.   M=2 S=1 L=0
6. I am trustworthy, and I comfortably depend on myself.   M=2 S=1 L=0
7. I don't seem to care what happens to me.   M=0 S=1 L=2
8. I am a self-confident person.   M=2 S=1 L=0
9. I easily become impatient with people.   M=0 S=1 L=2
10. I like myself, and I feel very comfortable with the way   M=2 S=1 L=0
    I am as a person.

11. I am afraid to be myself.	M=0 S=1 L=2
12. I am excited about myself and the potential that I have to develop as a person.	M=2 S=1 L=0
13. For me, anything is possible if I believe in myself.	M=2 S=1 L=0
14. I trust my ability to size up a situation.	M=2 S=1 L=0
15. I would describe myself as a creative person.	M=2 S=1 L=0
16. I effectively cope with the "ups" and "downs" of life.	M=2 S=1 L=0
17. I am comfortable revealing my weaknesses to my friends.	M=2 S=1 L=0
18. I am free to be myself and handle the consequences.	M=2 S=1 L=0
19. I feel in control of my life.	M=2 S=1 L=0
20. I accept my mistakes instead of bothering myself with them.	M=2 S=1 L=0
21. I regret many things I have done in the past.	M=0 S=1 L=2
22. I experience novelty and change in my daily life.	M=2 S=1 L=0
23. I am an open, honest, and spontaneous person.	M=2 S=1 L=0
24. I am regarded by others as a leader.	M=2 S=1 L=0
25. I form new friendships easily.	M=2 S=1 L=0

Stop and add your score. *(Max. score = 50)*   **TOTAL SCORE** _____

Transfer your score to the graph in Step B and to the appropriate profile on pages 173–174.

STEP B

Self-Awareness: Identify

Self-Esteem is an Intrapersonal skill that is essential to health, performance, and satisfaction in life and work. Self-Esteem is reflected by a genuine self-confidence, a high regard for self and others, and a sense of self-worth.

9 18 23 26 29	32 35 39	42 45 48 50
DEVELOP	STRENGTHEN	ENHANCE
You can benefit from learning about and understanding the Self-Esteem skill. Work through the lesson to fully develop this important Intrapersonal skill.	You currently identify the Self-Esteem skill as one that is at an average level of development. You can improve this skill and make it a strength.	You are claiming the Self-Esteem skill as a current strength. Continue to find ways to refine and enhance this important skill.

STEP C

Self-Knowledge: Understand

Self-esteem is not a trait or a fixed, stable construct. Positive Self-Esteem is developed and maintained daily by experiencing success after effectively dealing with yourself and the demands of living. It is a by-product of hopefulness and goal-directed behavior. Self-Esteem increases when you:

- Communicate clearly and directly (Assertion).
- Establish and maintain healthy relationships (Social Awareness).
- Accurately understand and accept differences in others (Empathy).
- Actively confront problems and decide on a course of action (Decision Making).
- Positively affect others (Positive Influence).
- Effectively manage yourself and your responsibilities (Time Management).
- Focus your energy appropriately to complete tasks (Drive Strength).
- Continue to pursue a task to completion (Commitment Ethic).
- Effectively manage the daily demands of living and working (Stress Management).
- Accurately identify and effectively express anger and anxiety (Anger and Anxiety Management).
- Model resilience and self-renewal (Positive Change).

Your Self-Esteem centers on your beliefs about your value as a person—your competence, your goodness, and your worth. The need to have positive (high) Self-Esteem is central to human motivation and behavior. Believing that you are a good person, that you can accomplish important goals, and that you deserve the trust and acceptance of others is basic to your emotional and physical health. Each time you effectively manage stress, constructively deal with anger, overcome fear, solve a problem, manage your responsibilities, or achieve a meaningful personal goal, you build positive Self-Esteem.

An active (intentional) attempt to understand your thoughts, feelings, and behaviors is the first step to building positive Self-Esteem. An awareness that behavior is what you do and not how you are as a person is necessary before you can accept your mistakes and remain resilient when dealing with personal setbacks and failed attempts to accomplish high standards. This awareness of Self and your ability to form a personal identity with an attached positive or negative value is a factor uniquely human.

Negative judgments and rejections of Self are associated with psychological pain and self-defeating behaviors. Positive evaluations—acceptance and affirmation—of Self are associated with good psychological health and productive living.

STEP D

Self-Development: Learn

An active attempt to understand yourself is the first step in developing a healthy relationship with yourself and others. Seeing yourself and your value as a person as being separate from your behavior is an understanding that allows you to be positive. This self-appreciation also affects, in a positive way, how you talk to yourself about yourself (self-talk).

Personal Self-Esteem means staying focused on your strengths (positive). This acceptance and acknowledgment of your strengths increases your optimism, constructive thinking, ability to let go of the past, self-worth, and ability to plan a better way to deal with the future. Learning to improve your Self-Esteem requires that you:

- Stay focused on your strengths.
- View a weakness as an indication that skill development and change are needed.
- Apply the Emotional Learning System and experiment with new ways of thinking and behaving.
- Demonstrate a willingness to challenge yourself by setting high goals.
- Acknowledge and appreciate the positive contributions of the emotional mind.
- Develop self-assertion and positive self-talk.

If I accept myself as I am, I change. If I accept another person as they are, they change.

CARL ROGERS

STEP E

Self-Improvement: Apply and Model

Learning to understand and constructively use your immediate experiences (thoughts or feelings) to select productive behaviors is the essence of emotionally intelligent behavior (wisdom). We have all heard that experience is

EXHIBIT 6.2	THE MOUNTAIN OF SELF-ESTEEM

the best teacher. Knowing how to learn from an immediate experience is a key to positive Self-Esteem.

Learning from past experiences is a traditional path to wisdom. Using your immediate experiences to learn and change is a key to feeling confident in the present and optimistic about your future. Explore the image in Exhibit 6.2 to see whether the thoughts and feelings it brings about are reflective of your Self-Esteem.

> To most . . . experience is like the stern lights of a ship, which illuminate only the track it has passed.
>
> COLERIDGE

Allow yourself to focus on the image of the mountain. Let the picture reflect your current thoughts and feelings about yourself. Continue to focus on the image and respond to the questions that follow.

1. As I focus on the image, the thoughts that I become aware of are:

_____

_____

_____

2. As I continue to focus on the picture and monitor my thoughts, I am most aware of feelings that I would label as:

_____

_____

_____

3. The thoughts underlying or associated with these feelings are:

_____

_____

_____

4. As I continue to focus on the picture and think about climbing the mountain, I think _____ and I feel

_____

Focusing on your immediate experiences allows you to become more aware of the thoughts and feelings that influence your behavior. How do your responses to the image reflect your level of self-esteem?

It is important to possess enough greatness of spirit to bear with the mistake of others.

I CHING

EXERCISE

Complete the following exercise and use it as you develop the Self-Esteem emotional skill into an intentional habit.

A. EXPLORE　How do you think, feel, and behave when you use this skill?

_____

_____

_____

Cognitive Focus:　Learning to value myself more

_____

_____

_____

Emotional Focus: Learning to feel better about myself

_____

_____

_____

Action Focus: Choosing to behave in ways that I respect and value

_____

_____

_____

B. IDENTIFY   Provide your personal definition of Self-Esteem.

_____

_____

_____

_____

_____

C. UNDERSTAND   Describe the importance of Self-Esteem.

_____

BENEFITS:

_____

_____

D. LEARN   Describe how to learn Self-Esteem.

_____

_____

_____

_____

_____

E. APPLY AND MODEL   List ways to practice.

_____

_____

_____

_____

EXHIBIT 6.3	EI SKILL: STRESS MANAGEMENT

STRESS MANAGMENT

If the pressure on you is too much and you get "stressed out," can you control your-self and keep your cool? Can you stay on top of your emotions and not get angry and up-tight? Stress management is the ability to handle stressful situations and keep doing what you need to do calmly and carefully to make things work right.

STRESS ISN'T ALWAYS A BAD THING. IF YOU HANDLE TOUGH SITUATIONS WELL, YOU WILL GROW AS A PERSON. AS IT IS SAID: "ORDEAL TEMPERS THE SOUL."

STRESS MANAGEMENT

Cognitive Focus: Learning to relax and calm myself

Emotional Focus: Feeling good about being important enough to relax

Action Focus: Choosing healthy behaviors and responses to stress

Definition

Positive Stress Management is the ability to choose and exercise healthy self-control in response to stressful events. This skill requires that you regulate the level of emotional intensity and use cognitive coping strategies during difficult and stressful situations. It is an essential emotional skill for health, perfor-mance, and satisfaction. *EI Man* discusses the importance of Stress Management in Exhibit 6.3.

EMOTIONAL INTELLIGENCE LESSON 13:
STRESS MANAGEMENT

STEP A

Self-Assessment: Explore

Read each statement, determine whether the statement applies to you Most Often (M), Sometimes (S), or Least Often (L), and circle the applicable letter–number combination.

1. Even though I have worked hard, I do not feel successful.   M=0 S=1 L=2

2. I cannot find the time to really enjoy life the way I would like.   M=0 S=1 L=2

3. I am bothered by physical symptoms, such as headaches, insomnia, ulcers, or hypertension.   M=0 S=1 L=2

4. When I see someone attempting to do something that I know I can do much faster, I get impatient.   M=0 S=1 L=2

5. I am a tense person.   M=0 S=1 L=2

6. I find it really difficult to let myself go and have fun.   M=0 S=1 L=2

7. I am not able to comfortably express strong emotions, such as fear, anger, and sadness.   M=0 S=1 L=2

8. If I really relaxed and enjoyed life the way I wanted to, I would find it hard to feel good about myself.   M=0 S=1 L=2

9. Even when I try to enjoy myself and relax, I feel a lot of pressure.   M=0 S=1 L=2

10. I often want people to speak faster and find myself wanting to hurry them up.   M=0 S=1 L=2

11. I am able to relax at the end of a hard day and go to sleep easily at night.   M=2 S=1 L=0

12. I often feel that I have little control over what I think, feel, and do.   M=0 S=1 L=2

13. I am unable to relax naturally and tend to rely on other things (e.g., drugs, alcohol, tobacco) to calm me down.   M=0 S=1 L=2

14. I feel tensed and pressured by the way I have to live.   M=0 S=1 L=2

15. My family and friends often encourage me to slow down and relax more.   M=0 S=1 L=2

16. I am impatient with myself and others, and I am usually pushing to hurry things up.   M=0 S=1 L=2

17. I am under so much stress that I can feel tension in my body.   M=0 S=1 L=2

18. My friends often say that I look worried, tense, or uptight.   M=0 S=1 L=2

19. I effectively deal with tension, and I have learned a variety of healthy ways to relax.   M=2 S=1 L=0

20. On the job, I work under a great deal of tension.   M=0 S=1 L=2

21. I have been unable to break negative habits that are a problem for me (e.g., drinking, smoking, overeating).   M=0 S=1 L=2

22. When I really relax and do absolutely nothing, I feel guilty about wasting time.   M=0 S=1 L=2

23. I have become extremely nervous and tense at times, and doctors have advised me to slow down and relax.   M=0 S=1 L=2

24. I seem to continually struggle to achieve and do well and seldom take time to honestly ask myself what I really want out of life.   M=0 S=1 L=2

25. I have developed relaxation techniques and practice them daily.   M=2 S=1 L=0

Stop and add your score. *(Max. score = 50)*   **TOTAL SCORE** _____

Transfer your score to the graph in Step B and to the appropriate profile on pages 173–174.

STEP B

Self-Awareness: Identify

Stress Management is an Intrapersonal skill that is essential to health, performance, and satisfaction in life and work. Stress Management is reflected by the ability to effectively control and manage stress and strong emotions.

4 9 14 19	24 29 34	39 44 49
DEVELOP	STRENGTHEN	ENHANCE
You can benefit from learning about and understanding the Stress Management skill. Work through the lesson to fully develop this important Intrapersonal skill.	You currently identify the Stress Management skill as one that is at an average level of development. You can improve this skill and make it a strength.	You are claiming the Stress Management skill as a current strength. Continue to find ways to refine and enhance this important skill.

STEP C

Self-Knowledge: Understand

Stress is the unavoidable by-product of the brain's response to any demand made on it. Positive stress management is a key factor in physical and mental health. We can improve our skill in managing stress by learning to use our "new" brain (thinking) when dealing with stressor events. In other words, we must develop coping strategies for specific stressors in our lives.

The "old" brain is capable of only two automatic responses when dealing with a stressor: fight (anger) and flight (fear). These old brain functions are involuntarily learned emotional responses to a perceived threat. The emotions of anger and fear are necessary for physical survival, and they serve protective functions. When the source of stress is psychologically threatening, not physically threatening, we can exercise control over the intensity and duration of our emotional reaction by learning to elicit a relaxation or calming response when faced by a stressful situation.

By learning and practicing relaxation, we can improve our ability to manage stress and improve our ability to perform productively and constructively when confronted by a stressor. Excessive hypertension, headaches, and sleep-onset insomnia are often related to stress management skill deficits.

Sources of stress include our own negative self-talk (intrapersonal), what other people do or say (interpersonal), and any change (environmental). If we know how to elicit relaxation in response to stress, we gain increased self-control over our thoughts, feelings, and behaviors.

Healthy and effective living in today's world requires the development of positive Stress-Management skills. The emotional intelligence model of a healthy personality assumes that anxiety and tension result from an inability to positively deal with intrapersonal, interpersonal, and environmental stress. To develop and strengthen your ability to deal with stress, complete the following five steps:

1. Develop a personal and operational definition of stress.
2. Identify your present level of the Stress Management emotional intelligence skill.
3. Identify specific sources of stress (personal stressors).
4. Develop specific personal skills to positively manage stress.
5. Implement a creative program of personal Stress-Management in your daily living.

Define stress. For most people living in our society, the major sources of personal stress are psychological, not physical. Hans Selye (1980) briefly defined stress as the nonspecific response of the body to any demand made on it. When you are required to adapt or adjust to any personal, interpersonal, or life situation, you experience stress. Any intrapersonal, interpersonal, or environmental event may be a personal stressor.

At the biological level, the body's response to stress is the same regardless of the type or nature of the stressor. The intensity of the demand for personal readjustment or adaptation is similar whether the stressing event is pleasant or unpleasant. Stress is a natural reaction to the demands of living and serves good and necessary purposes, but extreme or prolonged stress negatively affects us both physically and psychologically. Once we understand that stress is an unavoidable and necessary by-product of daily living, we can focus our attention on how to recognize our special and unique ways of responding to stress.

Identify current Stress-Management skill level. This step was accomplished when you completed the Emotional Intelligence Lesson 13 self-assessment. Recall how you scored as you complete the remaining steps.

Identify personal stressors. Psychological and physiological stress-related disorders have become a major health problem in our society. Stress-related origins may account for 50 to 80 percent of all diseases. Millions of people in our society are affected by hypertension, and millions more have sleep disturbances. Physical reactions related to stress include ulcers, bronchial asthma, hay fever, arthritis, hypertension, migraine headaches, drug abuse, insomnia, alcoholism, and mental health problems.

An individual's response to stress may be considered normal and adaptive when the response occurs to a source of stress that is identifiable, specific, and clear—once a person has reacted to the stressor, she quickly returns to a level of normal functioning. When the source of stress is ambiguous, undefined, or prolonged, the individual does not return to a normal mental and physiological level of functioning. Injurious stress reactions result when an individual increases normal stress to an excessive level for a prolonged period of time.

Personal well-being, academic achievement, and career effectiveness improve when a person learns and practices positive stress-management skills. An individual's reaction to life stressors can cause excessive personal anxiety and tension. The person experiences a loss of self-control. A person who automatically and constantly experiences strong emotions (fear, anger, sadness) and feels little or no personal control over the resulting thoughts, feelings, and behaviors is being damaged by stress. Difficulties with interpersonal communication, excessive and uncontrolled anger, a feeling of being unable to meet personal responsibilities, a perceived inability to make satisfying decisions, and an inability to effectively manage time are characteristics of negative psychological stress reactions.

Research has suggested that there is a significant connection between our ability to manage stress and our physical health. Review Exhibit 6.4 and become familiar with the characteristics of positive and negative stress management.

Self-destructive behavior patterns such as overeating, excessive drinking, and drug abuse may be indicative of stress reactions that gradually lead to physical destruction. In the Personal Skills Model, negative or self-destructive reactions to stress are considered indicative of specific personal skill deficits. The person moving toward healthier or skilled behaviors learns and develops new behaviors to positively manage stress.

By developing personal skills to positively manage stress, you can learn to alter your reaction to stressors. Physiologically, a person has a system for coping with stress similar to that found in animals. When people are subjected

EXHIBIT 6.4	PERSONAL SKILLS MODEL

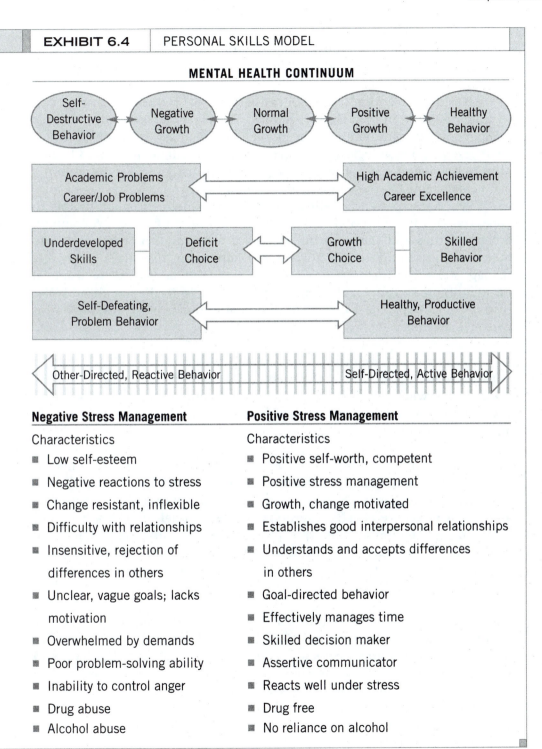

MENTAL HEALTH CONTINUUM

Self-Destructive Behavior ↔ Negative Growth ↔ Normal Growth ↔ Positive Growth ↔ Healthy Behavior

Academic Problems / Career/Job Problems ⟷ High Academic Achievement / Career Excellence

Underdeveloped Skills — Deficit Choice ⟷ Growth Choice — Skilled Behavior

Self-Defeating, Problem Behavior ⟷ Healthy, Productive Behavior

← Other-Directed, Reactive Behavior   Self-Directed, Active Behavior →

Negative Stress Management

Characteristics
- Low self-esteem
- Negative reactions to stress
- Change resistant, inflexible
- Difficulty with relationships
- Insensitive, rejection of differences in others
- Unclear, vague goals; lacks motivation
- Overwhelmed by demands
- Poor problem-solving ability
- Inability to control anger
- Drug abuse
- Alcohol abuse

Positive Stress Management

Characteristics
- Positive self-worth, competent
- Positive stress management
- Growth, change motivated
- Establishes good interpersonal relationships
- Understands and accepts differences in others
- Goal-directed behavior
- Effectively manages time
- Skilled decision maker
- Assertive communicator
- Reacts well under stress
- Drug free
- No reliance on alcohol

to major stress, they are aroused to a fight-or-flight reaction in the same way animals are. People can rarely deal with stress using the fight-or-flight response, and when they do, these behaviors are usually considered inappropriate in our society.

A person's perception of environmental stressors is a complicating factor in understanding human stress reactions. The psychological and emotional components of an individual's perception of an event also generate a physical stress response. Physiological stress reactions persist and are prolonged by negative psychological states. These prolonged and uninterrupted stress responses can be damaging to your physical and mental health.

When you experience feelings of being overwhelmed or are unable to cope, you are often immobilized by the anxiety caused by stress. A common aspect of stress and the resulting anxiety is a feeling of not being able to identify, understand, or control what is happening to you. To positively manage stress, you must develop an understandable and operational model for identifying stressors and clarifying your response to them. Exhibit 6.5 illustrates a three-part assessment process that you can use to identify your personal stressors.

Part 1: Identify the stressor event. The first step in identifying a source of stress is to understand and clarify the events that come before feeling anxious, tense, or overwhelmed. Body sensations and emotional reactions do not occur in a vacuum. When you feel tense or anxious, the feelings are reactions to a personal stressor.

Part 2: Identify any reactive thoughts, beliefs, and behaviors. Your thoughts, beliefs, and behaviors develop between the stressor event and the bodily and emotional consequences. How you talk to yourself (rationally or critically) and how you behave usually determine your emotional reactions. It is your individual perception and interpretation of the particular event. Once you clarify how you are creating your nonadaptive reactions to personal stressors, you can begin to change and control your emotional reactions by changing your thoughts and behaviors.

Part 3: Identify any bodily sensations and emotional reactions. People react differently to identical stressors, and it is important for you to be able to describe and clarify your emotional reactions, as well as assess the level and severity of your stress. Personal stress levels may vary from low to severe, and at times we can be incapacitated by severe stress reactions.

Once you understand how you are affected by specific personal stressors, you can learn to use specific Stress-Management skills to generate more adaptive and healthy reactions.

EXHIBIT 6.5	IDENTIFYING PERSONAL STRESSORS

PART 1:

Identify the Stressor Event

1. Date of event
2. Exact time
3. Location
4. What was I doing?
5. Who was with me?

PART 2:

Identify Any Reactive Thoughts, Beliefs, and Behaviors

6. What was I expecting to happen?
7. What images or memories came to mind?
8. What worries, concerns, or doubts did I have?
9. What was I saying to myself about the event? (Identify negative self-talk.)
10. What major beliefs or assumptions were related to the event? (Personal Belief System)
11. What was I talking about?
12. What did I actually *DO* in reaction to the event?

PART 3:

Identify Any Bodily Sensations and Emotional Reactions

13. What words (labels) best describe my bodily sensations and emotional reactions?

SELF-ASSESSED STRESS LEVEL

14. How severe are the feelings of stress that I experienced from this event?

LOW   SEVERE

1	2	3	4	5

EXAMPLE

PART 1:

Identify the Stressor Event

1. 12/12
2. 11:30 P.M.
3. Home in my room
4. Studying for final exam
5. By myself

PART 2:

Identify Any Reactive Thoughts, Beliefs, and Behaviors

6. I will study the wrong thing and fail like I did last time.
7. I remember how angry and embarrassed I was when the last test was returned.
8. If I don't improve, I will fail the test.
9. I'm stupid. There is no use in my studying anyway.
10. If I can't do well at anything, I'm a failure.
11. Myself
12. Gave up studying and went to bed

PART 3:

Identify Any Bodily Sensations and Emotional Reactions

13. Anxious, tense, angry
14. 4—severe stress

STEP D

Self-Development: Learn

Develop specific Stress-Management skills. Exhibit 6.6 lists certain items of the emotional intelligence components discussed thus far, potential stress sources, and recommended coping skills. Those recommended coping skills are described in this section.

Cognitive restructuring. The complexity of the human brain sets humans apart from the rest of the animal kingdom, and humans are often referred to as thinking animals. Humans are more than curious bipeds who go about making

EXHIBIT 6.6	STRESS SOURCES AND RECOMMENDED COPING SKILLS	
Emotional Component	**Stress Sources**	**Coping Skills**
Self-Esteem	Intrapersonal (thoughts)	Cognitive restructuring
Stress Management	Intrapersonal	Relaxation response
Social Awareness	Interpersonal (interaction with others, relationships)	Active listening
Empathy	Interpersonal	Empathic responding (internal frame of reference)
Assertion	Intrapersonal (self-inhibition)	Self-assertion
	Interpersonal (relationships)	Assertive communication
Drive Strength	Personal, academic, career demands, expectations, requirements	Action goal setting
Time Management	Personal, academic, career demands, conflicts	Time management
Decision Making	Personal, academic, career demands, conflicts	Problem solving
Anger Management	Intrapersonal, interpersonal, career/life demands	Anger management
Anxiety Management	Intrapersonal, interpersonal, career/life demands	Relaxation training
Positive Change	Intrapersonal—self-evaluation	Application of the Emotional Learning System

things, and most of us spend a great deal of time thinking about what we do or want to do. Most of our waking hours are filled by an endless sequence of thoughts, images, memories, expectations, and plans. What we say to ourselves in the privacy of our own heads makes a difference, and some psychologists have suggested that we are or become what we think.

Our cognition (thoughts or mental pictures) plays an important part in our behaviors and emotions. What and how we think influence what we feel and how we behave. Faulty cognition and negative self-talk lead to self-defeating behaviors and nonadaptive reactions to personal stressors. Many nonproductive and severe stress reactions are influenced by critical self-talk, perfection goals, irrational beliefs, and underdeveloped self-control skills. You can learn to identify and control what you think and then change the content of your thoughts and mental images to positively manage a specific stressor.

The Stress-Management skill required to change your thoughts and positively manage stress is called cognitive restructuring. Cognitive restructuring places an emphasis on the creative development of self-statements that are realistic, helpful, and related to specific and desired personal behavior changes. It is a self-management and self-change skill that allows you to become aware of your thinking processes, understand the effects that self-statements and beliefs have on your behavior and emotions, and learn how to change your reaction to personal stressors by having more helpful and rational thoughts.

Nonadaptive reactions to personal stressors are directly influenced by what you say to yourself (self-talk). If you realize that every event (stressor) in the real world is separated from your emotional reactions by thoughts, attitudes, and personal beliefs, you can begin to break up "automatic" responses by changing what you say to yourself—replace negative or self-defeating monologues with more realistic and helpful self-statements.

An example of how self-talk can influence an emotional reaction was presented in Exhibit 6.5. The person studying for the exam began to worry about studying the wrong material. This had actually happened in the past, and recalling the past experience caused the anxiety to increase. The critical self-statements followed: "I'm stupid" and "There is no use in my studying anyway." These negative self-statements increased the anxiety, and the student behaved accordingly by going to sleep instead of studying. You can positively manage stress by developing more appropriate self-statements. Positive self-statements are helpful because they specify the source of the stress, they are not self-critical monologues that increase anxiety, and they emphasize problem-solving behaviors that reduce the stressor's effect.

Now that you are aware of the importance of your thinking processes and self-talk in influencing your emotional reactions to personal stressors, you can learn to change your strong emotional reactions into milder ones by following the guidelines provided in Exhibit 6.7. Using this cognitive restructuring

EXHIBIT 6.7	COGNITIVE RESTRUCTURING PROCESS

Steps	**Self-Assessment Questions and Prerequisite Tasks for Change**
1. Identify the external event (Personal Stressor).	When? Where? What was I doing? Who was with me?
2. Identify your thoughts, beliefs, and behaviors.	I don't know what to study. I must do well. I'm stupid. There's no use studying anyway. I might as well give up and go to bed.
3. Describe, clarify, and assess your emotional stressor.	*Feelings:* anxious, uptight, angry, confused, helpless. *Body Sensations:* tight, tense.
4. Identify, dispute, and challenge *irrational* beliefs! Check catastrophic thinking and negative private mono-logues (critical self-talk).	*Examples of Core Irrational Beliefs:* 1. You *must* have sincere love and approval almost all of the time from significant people in your life. 2. You *should* be thoroughly competent, adequate, and perfect in everything you undertake. 3. Life is awful, terrible, or catastrophic when things do not go my way.
5. Create rational beliefs and substitute for irrational beliefs identified in Step 4. Develop and practice rational and personally helpful self-statements.	*Examples of Rational Beliefs:* 1. I would like approval from significant others, but I do *not need* such approval to be a good person. 2. I can be successful without demanding perfection of myself. 3. I can make my life enjoyable by changing how I handle frustration and stress.
6. Implement and practice the process of cognitive restruc-turing when dealing with personal stressors in your daily living. Focus on the task and set a personal behavioral goal to handle the problem.	I am scaring myself about failing when I really do not know what to study. I will talk to the teacher or a classmate, make sure that I know what material will be covered, and study for a minimum of 8 hours for the exam.

process may seem awkward when you initially begin to practice this new skill, but the benefits you gain will be reflected in your improved ability to manage stress and solve personal problems.

Relaxation skills. A variety of relaxation skills are briefly presented in the following section. Experiment with each of the skills, and think of the relaxation skill that you are willing to implement on a daily basis. No single relaxation skill "makes sense" or fits all individuals. Select a skill that fits you personally, and commit yourself to the idea of developing the skill to a level that will allow you to routinely and automatically use relaxation to live more creatively.

By developing a relaxation skill and using it daily, you will have the ability to elicit the relaxation in response to a personal stressor. This allows you to make more adaptive and healthier responses to stress and exercise increased self-control over potentially injurious stress situations. The personal energy and time required to learn and implement relaxation skills are excellent investments in your physical and mental health.

1. *Positive imagery.* You have an equal potential for using your imagination to create negative or positive feelings. You can achieve relaxation and positive feelings by recalling truly positive scenes from the past where you have felt security, safety, pride, happiness, joy, and confidence. Relaxing with positive imagery allows you to create positive feelings, use more of your potential for problem solving, and reduce tension and anxiety that may be inhibiting or self-defeating. Positive imagery can be used as a supplement to other relaxation skills. Visualizing a pleasant scene that is truly positive can deepen relaxation. The imagery is most effective if you create a scene that is positive and meaningful for you.

2. *Biofeedback training.* This involves the use of instrumentation to mirror back to the person what is going on underneath the skin. A person involved in biofeedback training receives immediate information about biological conditions such as muscle tension, skin surface temperature, brain wave activity, galvanic skin response, blood pressure, and heart rate. The purpose of the training is to teach the person how to voluntarily control these processes. Like all forms of relaxation, biofeedback training requires the motivation of the person and the skillful guidance of a trained professional. Through practice, a person can retain the skill of relaxation without a continual reliance on the instrumentation. A distinguishing feature of biofeedback training is that you can see or hear immediately the results of deep physical and mental relaxation. Biofeedback training has demonstrated effectiveness in positively altering stress-related reactions such as migraine or tension headaches, low back pain, and hypertension.

3. *Meditation.* Meditation as a relaxation skill for daily living has been practiced for over two thousand years. The acceptance and practice of meditation in our society has been increasing, and research evidence has indicated that the psychophysical states accompanying meditation seem incompatible with stress reaction. Pelletier (1977) provides an excellent treatment of meditation as a positive stress-management skill. All meditative techniques help induce a state of mental relaxation characterized by a slowing of breathing and heart rate, a decrease in the amount of oxygen consumed, and a lowering or stabilization of blood pressure. Regardless of the type practiced, meditation involves focusing your attention on relaxing thoughts and sensations, away from troubling, confusing, and stressful thoughts.

4. *Humor.* A good sense of humor is a personal stress skill worthy of daily practice. A sense of humor is usually considered characteristic of mental health, and the ability and willingness to laugh at events that are truly funny is an important stress-management skill. If you choose to find humor in yourself and life events, it is more difficult to be overwhelmed by dread and doom. The key to using humor to positively manage stress is the reframing of the stressful situation into a context that reduces personal anxiety.

5. *Communication techniques.* A person's primary communication style can either increase or decrease stress. Research has suggested that an assertive communication style in conflict situations is characteristic of positive stress management. Using interpersonal aggression or deference as primary communication styles causes an increase in personal stress and may lead to problematic behavior.

6. *Assertive training.* The assertive training model is based on three assumptions: a person's feelings and attitudes closely relate to actual behavior, a person's behavior is learned, and behavior can be changed through skills training. Assertive behavior has cognitive, affective (emotional), and behavioral aspects and is best learned in a small group under the supervision of a trained leader. Responsible assertive behavior that is personally satisfying without violating another person's rights is the goal of assertion training.

STEP E

Self-Improvement: Apply and Model

Implement a personal stress-management program. It is now time to try some of the stress-reduction techniques discussed earlier. To practice the cognitive restructuring technique, identify a recent event that caused you to experience a great deal of stress. Then, work your way through the steps in Exhibit 6.8.

EXHIBIT 6.8	COGNITIVE RESTRUCTURING EXERCISE

Steps	Self-Assessment Questions and Prerequisite Tasks for Change
1. Identify the external event (Personal Stressor).	
2. Identify your thoughts, beliefs, and behaviors.	
3. Describe, clarify, and assess your emotional stressor.	
4. Identify, dispute, and challenge *irrational* beliefs! Check catastrophic thinking and negative private monologues (critical self-talk).	
5. Create rational beliefs and substitute for irrational beliefs identified in Step 4. Develop and practice rational and personally helpful self-statements.	
6. Implement and practice the process of cognitive restructuring when dealing with personal stressors in your daily living. Focus on the task and set a personal behavioral goal to handle the problem.	

Before you begin to practice the relaxation techniques, use the following suggestions to make the relaxation exercises maximally beneficial:

■ Before beginning a relaxation exercise, estimate your level of stress and tension using a SUD (Subjective Units of Disturbance) Scale.

RELAXED   TENSE

0	25	50	75	100

Zero signifies that you are completely relaxed with *no* tension. The other end of the scale, 100, indicates complete tension. Subjectively estimate your current level of tension on the SUD Scale before beginning a relaxation exercise.

■ Select a relaxation script, and arrange yourself and your physical surroundings to be conducive to relaxation. During the first few sessions of relaxation training, the room should be quiet and dimly lighted—no glaring lights. An earphone for your cassette recorder may be used for more privacy. Sit in a comfortable chair or lie down in a comfortable position. A recliner armchair with a footrest is ideal. Arrange yourself comfortably so that 15 to 25 minutes can be devoted to the relaxation exercise. A completely reclined position should be avoided. Your head should be propped up to avoid going to sleep.

■ Your clothing should be as comfortable as possible. Any jacket or coat, as well as shoes, should be removed before sitting in the chair. Tight-fitting clothes should be loosened. Sit with your back flat against the chair, your arms and hands resting comfortably on the arms of the chair or in your lap, and your feet resting side-by-side and slightly apart. Feet or legs should be uncrossed.

■ It is easier to listen and relax if you allow your eyes to close as soon as you get yourself seated as comfortably as you can. Ensure that you are not disturbed by phone calls or external distractions.

■ Use the relaxation exercise to study what happens to your tension as you become more and more relaxed. Focus on the words and instructions during the exercise, and really allow yourself to participate in relaxing your muscles, hearing and feeling the instructions, and vividly creating the suggested images.

■ Practice the relaxation exercise that works best for you daily. The exercises are not presented as rituals that you must do. Completing the exercise is a source of relaxation. Two or three weeks of daily practice will move you closer to developing the relaxation response. Self-training in relaxation builds self-control of feeling states.

■ Keep a personal relaxation record. Use the SUD Scale before and after each relaxation exercise. Record the level you achieve each time. With practice, you will lower your SUD level and learn more and more about how to reduce your stress. When you are able to consistently achieve the relaxation response, you may prefer to practice the exercises only when you feel the need.

The next exercise involves the positive imagery relaxation technique. Have someone read the passage from Exhibit 6.9 while you listen and relax.

| **EXHIBIT 6.9** | POSITIVE IMAGERY RELAXATION |

Seat or recline yourself comfortably. Get as comfortable as you can. Allow your eyes to close and relax. . . . Take in a slow breath. . . . Hold it for a few seconds. . . . Release it slowly and notice the relaxed feeling change in your chest. Allow yourself to be calm, relaxed, and peaceful. With each breath, you become more deeply relaxed, quiet, and at peace with yourself.

Focus on the words I say, and allow your mind to create the images as I describe them. This is an exercise of positive imagery, a creation of pleasant thoughts and feelings, a way of relaxing completely and deeply.

You are sitting comfortably on a clean, white beach. You look out at the blue-green water and watch as the white-capped waves move toward the shore. . . . You are deeply relaxed and calm, finding peace with yourself.

You can feel the warmth of the sun on your skin and the movement of the wind as your relaxation becomes deeper and deeper. In the distance you can hear the call of a seabird and the sound of the waves constantly meeting the shore.

The sky is a brilliant blue and cottonlike clouds seem motionless about the horizon. The whiteness of the clouds and the blueness of the sky area contrast with the moving water. You are deeply relaxed and at peace with yourself, quiet and calm with comfortable feelings. Time passes quickly as you become more and more relaxed.

The sun is beginning to set, and its fading light is red as it begins to disappear behind the dunes. You can feel a chill as the evening breeze blows cooler and the last rays of light from the sun are absorbed by the dark.

You become more deeply relaxed as you gaze into the flames of the open fire burning in front of you. You can hear the sounds of the burning wood and the smell of the fire fills the air. The changing colors of the fire are red, blue, and purple, and the wood burns ash white. Sparks float up and disappear as the wind cools them. You are calm, relaxed, and at peace with yourself.

The sound of the waves, the coolness of the breeze, and the light of the rising moon relax and calm you. Your thoughts are calm, pleasant, and peaceful. You relax totally and enjoy the peaceful feeling and relaxation that you have given yourself.

At the count of three, I want you to open your eyes feeling refreshed and full of energy. 1 – 2 – 3.

Using your imagination and creativity, write your own relaxation script. Pick a scene that you like best—one in which you feel peaceful, safe, happy, and relaxed. Remember to use all five senses—sight, sound, touch, smell, and taste. Make an audiotape from the script and listen to the tape daily.

EXERCISE

Complete the following exercise and use it as you develop the Stress Management emotional skill into an intentional habit.

A. EXPLORE   How do you think, feel, and behave when you use this skill?

_____

_____

_____

Cognitive Focus: Learning to relax and calm myself

_____

_____

_____

Emotional Focus: Feeling good about being important enough to relax

_____

_____

_____

Action Focus: Choosing healthy behaviors and responses to stress

_____

_____

_____

B. IDENTIFY   Provide your personal definition of Stress Management.

_____

_____

_____

_____

C. UNDERSTAND   Describe the importance of Stress Management.

_____

BENEFITS: _____

_____

D. LEARN Describe how to learn Stress Management.

_____

_____

_____

_____

_____

E. APPLY AND MODEL List ways to practice.

_____

_____

_____

_____

_____

LINK

The final chapter presents an expanded view of personal excellence and emphasizes the systems, principles, and skills that you must balance to feel harmony and act wisely. A model of self-renewal is presented to help you learn a process to renew yourself and become more resilient.

Academic and Career Success Planner Activities

ACTIVITY 6.1	STRESS MANAGEMENT HINTS FOR HIGH ACHIEVEMENT

Stress Management

- Establish and maintain positive and protective relationships that encourage you to succeed.

- Sleep, relax, play, exercise, eat and drink wisely.

- Laugh as much as you can at things that are truly funny.

- When emotions (anger, fear and sadness) are too strong for too long, identify and label the emotions correctly (i.e., "I am angry.") Accept responsibility for responding to the emotion. Decide if and how you want to express the emotion so as not to hurt yourself or others.

- Use the EI Academic Success Planner to organize and prioritize academic and work obligations. Set and accomplish daily goals that are both meaningful and fun. Balance your day to include rest and relaxation.

ACTIVITY 6.2	YOUR STRESS MANAGEMENT CALENDAR FOR HIGH ACHIEVEMENT

Month_____ Year _____

EI Skills Focus:

Stress Management

The ability to relax naturally by using successful stress management skills daily. Performance improves in stressful situations.

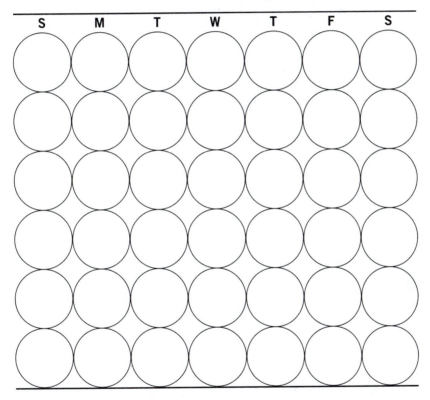

Will Do Behaviors: Stress Management

Priority	When	Target Date
1. _____	1. _____	1. _____
2. _____	2. _____	2. _____
3. _____	3. _____	3. _____
How important?	How Urgent?	Completion Date

CHAPTER 7

Self-Renewal and Personal Excellence

As a student–mentor, I can say that Mentoring with Emotional Intelligence has been very instrumental in achieving significant milestones and breakthroughs. By applying the principles of EI, I was able to adapt to different situations that presented difficult challenges. I have learned that if I display confidence and use the other EI skills, then my protégé will be more receptive and more likely to trust and accept what I am teaching. The success of the mentor and the whole mentoring process, therefore, depend greatly on one's personal understanding and the practice of Emotional Intelligence each and every day.

STUDENT–MENTOR
*Tshwane University of Technology,
Pretoria, South Africa*

Preview

The emotional intelligence skills that you have identified, learned, and practiced will improve your academic and career success. With continued practice, these new behaviors will become more comfortable and automatic for you on an individual level. We refer to these new behaviors as intentional success habits. In this final chapter, we emphasize the importance of your individual commitment to excellence and present a model for lifelong learning and self-renewal.

Self-renewal is a continuous and daily process of applying the Emotional Learning System to behave wisely, think constructively, and feel confident in your ability to accurately identify and express emotions. When you are in the presence of a person who models energy, excitement, interest, and vitality, you are witness to the results of self-renewal. If there is a key to staying forever young, it lies in a person's ability to positively manage stress, personal change, and the demands and crises of daily living and working.

Personal excellence is the process of developing yourself into the best person you can be, and self-renewal is the self-directed personal change process that allows you to maintain high levels of achievement, happiness, and physical health. To this end, we have emphasized emotional intelligence skills as behaviors—ways of doing. Now, it is time to expand the view of the person to include ways of believing and being. The focus of this chapter is on an integrated view of the person that includes the beliefs and interactive systems that move one toward excellence, balance, harmony, and wisdom.

THOUGHTS ABOUT EXCELLENCE AND SELF-RENEWAL

We want you to think about how people build excellence, high achievement, and personal satisfaction into their lives. We have described the essence of this process as developing emotional intelligence and building quality from within. As we begin, you may want to challenge how you think about yourself as a person and open your mind to the possibility of change and self-renewal.

Here are some thoughts to challenge your way of thinking about yourself and your possibilities for high achievement.

1. John Dewey said long ago that human nature exists and operates in an environment—it is not "in" that environment as coins are in a box, but as a plant is in the sunlight and soil. Unlike plants, healthy, high-achieving people who live quality lives have to nurture and renew themselves in environments that are often not growth oriented. People who achieve excellence are positive and active. Negative belief systems and emotional reactivity erode personal excellence and productivity.

2. Think of yourself as a system instead of an individual. You have relationships with Self, with others, and with the environment. Interdependence is the best descriptor of a productive and healthy relationship. Independence is

incomplete, and codependence is self-defeating. Excellence is a highly personalized and internal process. Achievement and success are personally defined. Achieving and succeeding are more processes than arrival states. One cannot fail unless one hopes or strives for more than it is possible to achieve. Succeeding and failing are very close and parallel processes involving cognitive, emotional, and behavioral components. Hope and optimism are key elements in achieving excellence.

3. Excellence is a by-product of achieving personally meaningful goals that are congruent with your core beliefs and values. No one sees the world, perceives reality, learns, expresses their emotions, and chooses their behavior in the same way that you do. The focus of this chapter is on your uniqueness. Our major goal is to help you understand the principles, systems, and skills that you can use to achieve excellence in your life and your work.

4. People have two ways of knowing and experiencing the world. One system is rational and analytical. The other system is experiential and intuitive. Our focus has been on the development of emotional intelligence—how to make positive changes in the emotional system that leads to increased productivity and personal excellence.

PERSONAL EXCELLENCE

Personal excellence is a process of becoming the best person one can be and is reflected in how one is, as well as what one does. Personal excellence is indicated in people who develop their gifts and talents to the fullest, achieving a harmony in how they think, feel, behave, and believe that leads to productive relationships and outcomes. Rather than an arrival state, personal excellence is a journey of positive development beyond one's self. It manifests in self-defined and self-valued achievements that reflect one's best efforts. The EI centric theory of personal excellence connects the process of building quality from within with the lived experience of each individual.

RICHARD HAMMETT, 2007

Your beliefs about yourself are key factors in high achievement and the development of personal excellence. When you value and appreciate yourself as a unique person and your behaviors are congruent with your most important values, you can develop a sense of meaning and purpose. Once you are clear about your purpose and are confident in your abilities, you can create a guiding vision that leads you to higher levels of achievement and personal satisfaction.

Achievement drive increases when you are committed to and focused on a meaningful purpose, develop clear personal goals to guide your daily behaviors, and accept personal responsibility for your actions and choices. Beliefs give you purpose, vision gives you guidance, and commitment gives you the positive energy and power to reach high levels of personal achievement and excellence.

Managing change and developing positive support systems are important factors in high levels of personal achievement and excellence. Change-management skills provide balance and stability. You can stay focused, in balance, and on-task when you are able to positively manage stress and actively confront and solve problems. Interdependence involves living and working cooperatively with others. Healthy interpersonal relationships support your individual efforts to achieve, as well as buffer you from the negative aspects of distress and failure.

Personal excellence is the by-product of a confluence of interactive systems, principles, and skills. The core belief is that we each have value and worth as a person and that our contributions make a positive difference in the world. *EI Man's* description of personal excellence is provided in Exhibit 7.1.

| **EXHIBIT 7.1** | *EI MAN'S* TAKE ON PERSONAL EXCELLENCE |

Personal Excellence

Personal Excellence, for the person who practices the skills of Emotional Intelligence, becomes a way of life for her or him. Once these skills have been learned and practiced for a length of time, which varies with different people, they form into habits.

And just as a negative habit can erode you and wear you down, so can a positive habit build you up and make you a stronger, more positive and more productive person.

When you go to learn a new skill, oftentimes it seems easy at the start. Persist and it becomes much more difficult, tedious and you wonder why you ever started this nonsense. Persevere even more, and suddenly you "break free" and the new skill becomes automatic and you flow with it without thinking about it.

The first time you do this is usually the most trying, the next time is easier, and so on and on. The learning curve for Emotional Intelligence skills lessens more and more as you proceed on the road of Personal Excellence.

> PERSONAL EXCELLENCE IS ACHIEVED BY NEVER ACCEPTING WHAT YOU ARE AS COMPLETE AND PERFECT; BUT ALWAYS READY TO CHANGE FOR THE BETTER. THEN YOU WILL NEVER STOP GROWING.

SYSTEMS, PRINCIPLES, AND SKILLS

The process of developing excellence in our lives and work can be conceptualized as five distinct, but interactive, systems: beliefs, guidance, power, support, and balance. Each system supports a principle that encompasses particular skills. Exhibit 7.2, Personal Excellence, illustrates the interconnectedness of these systems, principles, and skills (Hammett, 2007).

EXHIBIT 7.2	A FRAMEWORK OF PERSONAL EXCELLENCE

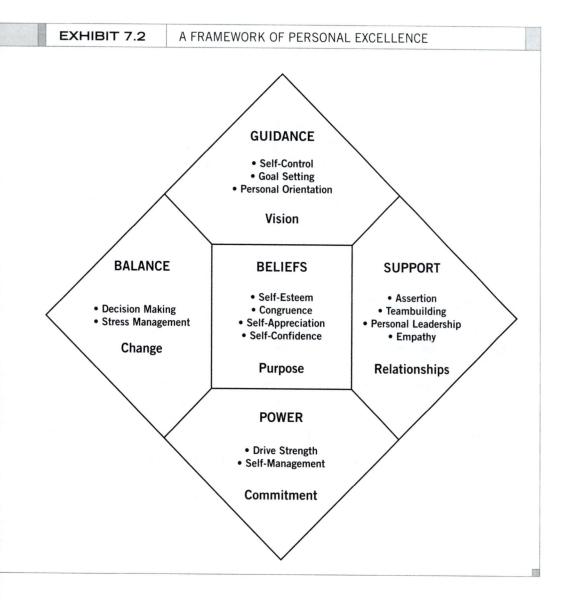

GUIDANCE
- Self-Control
- Goal Setting
- Personal Orientation

Vision

BALANCE
- Decision Making
- Stress Management

Change

BELIEFS
- Self-Esteem
- Congruence
- Self-Appreciation
- Self-Confidence

Purpose

SUPPORT
- Assertion
- Teambuilding
- Personal Leadership
- Empathy

Relationships

POWER
- Drive Strength
- Self-Management

Commitment

The Belief System

This system is the core or inner system that contains the ideas and views (words and pictures) of the things you can achieve. Your beliefs influence what you attempt to do, how much you do, and how well you do. Without clear values, confidence in your abilities, and a basic appreciation of your potential to succeed, you are bound by the history of your past and reinforced by your habits in the present. Optimistic beliefs expand your potential to achieve beyond your normal expectations.

The belief system is concerned with the principle of *purpose* and functions to define your levels of achievement and excellence. Your belief system influences your view of what you are capable of achieving. The core belief is that you have positive value as a person. Self-confidence and meaningful values are a part of your personal belief system. The key skills within this principle are

1. *Self-Esteem*—your learned ability to view yourself as positive, competent, and successful in achieving personal goals.

2. *Congruence*—your learned ability to clarify important values related to your goals and beliefs, as well as your alignment of behaviors and choices for self-development related to values, goals, and beliefs.

3. *Self-Confidence*—your learned ability to focus on competence and feel positive about your potential to perform effectively.

4. *Self-Appreciation*—your learned ability to value yourself positively and to be in touch with your strengths as a person.

The Guidance System

The guidance system guides your future achievement, growth, and change. It is the teleological dimension within you—the dimension that lets you anticipate and plan your future in ways that you choose instead of simply reacting or orienting yourself to the demands of the external environment.

The guidance system is concerned with the principle of *vision*. A unique human quality is the ability to consider the future and to formulate goals that influence your present behavior. The key skills within this principle are

1. *Self-Control*—your learned ability to exercise choice and control over the strength of your emotional response. This skill is essential for high achievement and functions to keep you focused on your goals.

2. *Goal Setting*—your learned ability to set clear and specific personal goals. Achievable goals provide a focus for personal motivation.

3. *Personal Orientation*—your learned ability to see yourself as a positive person with the potential to continually learn and change.

The Power System

This system supplies your energy and ability to move forward to do productive work. The power system is internal and closely related to the beliefs system. Achievement drive is increased by expanding beliefs (mental paradigms) and setting value-congruent goals.

The power system is concerned with the principle of *commitment* and functions to supply and direct energy for goal achievement. Motivation is internal and committed; focused energy leads to high levels of personal achievement and excellence. The key skills within this principle are

1. *Drive Strength*—your learned ability to persist and accomplish personal goals that are meaningful and satisfying.
2. *Self Management*—your learned ability to manage your life and responsibilities proactively.

The Balance System

This system provides harmony and functions to create a confluence of clear goals, important values, expanded beliefs, adequate support, and focused energy and power. A major function of the balance system is to positively manage change in the present.

The balance system is concerned with the principle of *change* and functions to maintain balance in your achievements and consistency in your performance. The key skills within this principle are

1. *Decision Making*—your learned ability to be decisive and make good choices.
2. *Stress Management*—your learned ability to positively manage stress while keeping yourself physically and emotionally healthy.

The Support System

This system is your connection to others through relationships. It holds you up by supplying synergy from people who accept and care about you when you lose touch with your ability to do that for yourself. Social awareness, empathy, and assertion help establish and maintain your support system. Close relationships with others affirm your value, buffer distress, and enrich your life with a protective and natural interdependence.

The support system is concerned with the principle of *relationships* and functions to provide support from others. Positive support from others and cooperative interpersonal relationships foster high levels of personal achievement. The key skills within this principle are

1. *Assertion*—your learned ability to communicate your needs and wants to others in a direct and honest manner.
2. *Team Building*—your learned ability to add synergy and contribute constructively in cohort activities.
3. *Personal Leadership*—your learned ability to influence and affect others in positive ways.
4. *Empathy*—your learned ability to accurately understand the thoughts and feelings of others.

The healthy, productive person is goal directed. High achievement and personal excellence are by-products of a goal-directed system of focused energy, positive beliefs, supportive relationships, and congruent values. The five systems are interactive, so balance and congruence are essential elements.

What all this means at a basic and personal level is that you are enough and have everything within you to be happy and productive. If you want to grow and change, move toward higher levels of achievement, and strive for academic and career excellence, begin by setting personal goals that move you into dimensions of behavior that are new, interesting, and meaningful.

EMOTIONAL SKILLS PROFILE

The Emotional Skills Assessment Process (ESAP) lessons that you completed in Chapters 3 through 6 provided you with a self-assessment of your current development level of 10 powerful emotional intelligence skills and 3 potential problem areas that should be converted to the appropriate emotional skill for each area. These emotional skills are important in four competency areas: Interpersonal, Leadership, Self-Management, and Intrapersonal.

Transfer (you may already have done this) your total scores from **Step A. Self-Assessment: Explore** for each of the emotional intelligence lessons to the Emotional Skills Profile on the following page. Each of the 13 emotional intelligence skills on your profile has a series of numbers to the right of each scale. These raw scores show where your total scores on each skill should be marked. For example, if your total score on Assertion is 24, you will place a dot or circle that number.

If you want to see how your score compares with those of other college students, look at the **Standard Scores** at the top of the profile. The score of 24 on Assertion would be equal to a standard score of 50. This means that your score on Assertion is in the average or expected range when compared to those of other college students. Scores to the right (Enhance) indicate your perceived strengths. Scores to the left (Develop) indicate skills to learn and practice.

High scores on Aggression, Deference, and Change Orientation indicate potential problems and the need for skill development. Aggression needs to be converted to the emotional skill of Anger Management; Deference needs to be converted to the emotional skill of Anxiety Management; Change Orientation needs to be converted to the emotional skill of Positive Change.

Accurate and current self-knowledge is powerful. Emotional learning and emotional intelligence skills use a person's internal frame of reference as the basis of the learning process. Positive Change is an intentional, self-directed process that is supported by emotional skills and commitment. Two steps make change positive and personally meaningful: Obtaining important and useful emotional knowledge about Self, and developing emotional skills that guide and support lifelong emotional learning.

EMOTIONAL SKILLS PROFILE

Standard Score	Develop	Strengthen	Enhance
Part I: Interpersonal Skills			
Assertion	9 12 15 18	21 24 27	30 33 36
Part II: Leadership Skills			
Social Awareness	5 7 9 11 13	15 17 19	21 23 24
Empathy	6 8 10 12 14	16 18 20	22 24
Decision Making	5 8 10 12	14 16 18	20 22 24
Positive Influence	4 6 9 11	13 15 17	19 21 24
Part III: Self-Management Skills			
Drive Strength	10 14 18 22 26	30 34 38	42 44 46 50
Commitment Ethic	8 10 12 14	16 18 20	22 24
Time Management	5 8 10 12	14 16 18	20 22 24
Part IV: Intrapersonal Skills			
Self-Esteem	9 18 23 26 29	32 35 39	42 45 48 50
Stress Management	4 9 14 19	24 29 34	39 44 49
SCALE	**DEVELOP**	**STRENGTHEN**	**ENHANCE**

Standard Score scale: 15 20 25 30 35 40 45 50 55 60 65 70 75 80 85

A Profile of Potential Problem Areas			
Aggression (Convert to Anger Management skill)	2 4 6	8 11 15	19 24 28 35
Deference (Convert to Anxiety Management skill)	2 4 6 10	14 18 22	26 30 32 36
Change Orientation (Convert to Positive Change)	1 3 5 7	9 11 13	16 18 21 24
SCALE	**LOW**	**NORMAL**	**HIGH**

PERSONAL EXCELLENCE INVENTORY

Estimate your progress toward Personal Excellence by reading each of the 150 success behaviors and indicating whether or not the statement is True (T) or False (F) for you now. Add up the number of statements that you marked as True, and circle the number to mark your spot on the Continuum of Excellence that follows the inventory.

_____ I write down clear personal and work-related goals to guide my achievement.

_____ I can quickly calm myself when something upsets me.

_____ I feel a harmony between who I am and what I do.

_____ I am comfortable when meeting new people.

_____ I organize my daily responsibilities into an effective personal time schedule.

_____ I am committed to developing my full potential as a person.

_____ I am a good decision maker.

_____ I am confident in my ability to successfully perform tasks assigned to me.

_____ I have a good ability to really listen to another person and accurately understand what he is feeling.

_____ I am a dependable person.

_____ I can hold my own and effectively deal with persuasive people.

_____ I face problems rather than avoid them.

_____ I am optimistic when I think about what I will accomplish in my life and work.

_____ I can refuse a request from an important person when my values say no.

_____ I set and accomplish specific goals daily.

_____ I have developed the skill to picture my goals clearly in my mind's eye.

_____ After experiencing a stressful event, I have a routine to minimize its effect.

_____ Visualizing my important goals creates positive feelings for me.

_____ I know how close I can stand to another person without making her uncomfortable.

_____ I complete my daily responsibilities within specific time frames.

_____ I form and keep very close friendships with several people.

_____ I make decisions quickly with good results.

_____ I achieve positive results from my work efforts.

_____ I manage myself well when dealing with the emotions of others.

_____ People turn to me when something really needs to get done.

_____ I can control my own anger when someone is really upset with me.

_____ In a problem situation, I generate several alternatives and effectively evaluate options.

_____ I value myself and my contributions to life and work.

_____ When dealing with important issues, I am direct and honest in saying what I think or feel.

_____ When working toward a goal, I regularly evaluate my progress and obtain feedback from others.

_____ I write down specific strategies to help me achieve my goals.

_____ I do not spend time or energy worrying about things that I cannot control.

_____ My inner Self is pleased with the goals that I have set.

_____ Other people find me easy to talk to.

_____ I complete my work assignments on time.

_____ I am trustworthy and I can comfortably depend on myself.

_____ I have established a personal process for making important decisions.

_____ I know my strengths as a person and can use them fully when needed.

_____ I can ask questions without making the other person defensive or uncomfortable.

_____ I will work day and night to complete a project that I have agreed to do.

_____ I do not get manipulated into doing things I do not want to do.

_____ I am a good problem solver.

_____ I accept responsibility for my choices and actions.

_____ I ask directly for what I need and want from others.

_____ I challenge myself by setting goals that lead to high levels of achievement.

_____ I use positive thoughts and images to expand my beliefs about my ability to attain high goals.

_____ I have learned relaxation skills and practice them daily.

_____ I feel worthy of receiving the benefits from the goals that I have set.

_____ I get along very well with people.

_____ I can focus on what I need to do and waste no time.

_____ My behavior is positive and self-affirming.

_____ When I face a difficult decision, I am good at creating alternatives and making a priority choice.

_____ I view failure as an important lesson from which to learn.

_____ I am a good listener.

_____ I have a strong and clear sense of right and wrong for myself, and I behave accordingly.

_____ I can express my anger constructively when I am mad at someone.

_____ When problem solving, I know how and when to seek feedback from others.

_____ I am very confident in my abilities as a person.

_____ I use good verbal skills to clarify confusing communications from others.

_____ I direct and focus my energy on accomplishing important goals.

_____ I continually learn new skills that I need to achieve my goals.

_____ I have good control over strong emotions like anger and fear.

_____ I am comfortable thinking about being prosperous and successful.

_____ Other people quickly trust me.

_____ I know precisely how much time to allow for completing work tasks.

_____ I have a good sense of humor that hurts no one.

_____ When faced with an important decision, I am not anxious about making a wrong choice.

_____ I accept personal responsibility for what I choose to do or not to do.

_____ I can allow another person to be upset or angry without getting defensive.

_____ I have a solid feeling of confidence in my ability to create a successful life for myself.

_____ Strong emotions never interfere with the quality of my performance.

_____ Others ask my help in solving problems.

_____ I am a good leader.

_____ Others appreciate and value my ability to provide direct and accurate feedback.

_____ I know and use an effective process of daily goal setting.

_____ I review and revise my goals as I work to achieve them.

_____ When I am stressed about a problem, I can talk it through and solve it.

_____ I share my prosperity with others.

_____ I am an effective communicator.

_____ I regularly schedule personal time for rest and renewal.

_____ I am a healthy person and take good care of myself physically and emotionally.

_____ The outcomes of my decisions are considered "good" by others.

_____ I believe that I am a valuable person.

_____ I accept and work well with people who are very different from me.

_____ I live my life in line with my personal values.

_____ I rarely get angry about things I cannot control or change.

_____ I have the ability to solve problems that stump others.

_____ I like myself and am comfortable with how I am as a person.

_____ I bring up criticisms or complaints when I feel that it is important to do so.

_____ I prefer to work on challenging goals that offer some risk of failure.

_____ I break down my goals into small steps that I can accomplish daily.

_____ Worry does not keep me from quickly falling asleep.

_____ I deserve abundance when I create abundance for others.

_____ I can like someone and strongly disagree with his opinions.

_____ When evaluated by others, I receive high marks for effectively managing my assignments and responsibilities.

_____ I change and develop myself by being open to new ideas.

_____ Coworkers ask for my help when making important decisions.

_____ I succeed in achieving my personal goals.

_____ I get my ideas and opinions across without dominating or discrediting the other person.

_____ I do very well in any new area that I try.

_____ When I really get angry, I know how to calm myself down.

_____ I have a good ability to select the best solution from many alternatives.

_____ I am optimistic when I think about what I can accomplish in my life and work.

_____ I comfortably accept praise from others.

_____ I know my weaknesses and consider their effect when working toward an important goal.

_____ When I develop a new goal, I set a specific time to achieve it.

_____ I am patient with people with whom I disagree.

_____ The more I give to others, the more fulfilled I am.

_____ I make friends with many different kinds of people.

_____ I can effectively work on and complete several assignments at the same time with good results.

_____ I am excited about myself and the potential that I have as a person.

_____ I am decisive when a crisis calls for a quick decision.

_____ I feel control over how I feel and behave.

_____ I have the ability to accurately see things from the other person's perspective.

_____ People admire my ability to successfully accomplish what I set out to do.

_____ I can think my way through strong feelings and behave effectively.

_____ Under pressure, I am decisive and act quickly to solve problems.

_____ I stand up for myself when challenged or opposed by an important person.

_____ When annoyed, I bring it up directly with the other person involved.

_____ I enjoy goals that require me to make intensive, long-term commitments.

_____ I use messages, words, and pictures to focus on achieving my goals.

_____ I feel relaxed more than I feel tense or anxious.

_____ My goals, values, beliefs, and convictions are in harmony.

_____ What I say or do does not make others uncomfortable.

_____ I do not feel pressured from trying to catch up on things that I should have completed in the past.

_____ I view myself as a creative person.

_____ I seldom regret the decisions that I have made.

_____ I feel in control of my life.

_____ I have an excellent ability to work cooperatively with others.

_____ Even when I encounter personal difficulties, I complete assignments and obligations on time.

_____ I have learned to control and constructively express strong emotions.

_____ I am rarely blocked or stuck by difficult problems.

_____ I easily give and receive compliments.

_____ When talking with superiors, I express my views and concerns in a clear and direct way.

_____ When working on a goal, I can concentrate and complete tasks requiring long periods of intense effort.

_____ I set goals that I can see and experience in terms of end results.

_____ I stop myself from replaying self-defeating thoughts.

_____ I choose behaviors that are consistent with my most important values.

_____ I can accurately judge my impact on others.

_____ I consistently work on high priority tasks first during my most productive time of day.

_____ I challenge and renew myself by learning about new ideas and skills.

_____ I am viewed as a decisive person.

_____ I effectively manage problems and difficult situations.

_____ People sense that I understand and care about their thoughts and feelings.

_____ When I decide to do something, I follow through until I complete the job.

_____ I do not come on too strong and overpower others with my opinions.

_____ As a member of a group problem-solving effort, my suggested solutions are considered valuable.

_____ I stay positive about my value as a person even when my achievement is down.

_____ I compliment others for their contributions.

_____ I finish what I start and can be counted on to do my part in completing a task.

CONTINUUM OF EXCELLENCE

Understanding and applying the Emotional Learning System is a beginning step in developing personal excellence. If you persist in your efforts to develop and enhance emotional intelligence skills, they can make a lasting and very positive difference in your life. You are responsible for deciding how much effort to put forth to realize your personal goals. We each make choices daily that either move us toward problematic interpersonal interactions and relationships or move us toward excellence.

As a means of estimating your progress toward personal excellence, record your score from the Personal Inventory on the Continuum of Excellence.

Continuum of Excellence

0	50	75	100	150

Self-Destructive	Self-Defeating	Positive/Enhancing	Excellence
Academic failure	Underachievement	Academic achievement	High achievement
No productive work	Change indicated	Productive work	High-quality work
No apparent direction	Unclear direction	Goal oriented	Goal directed
Numerous problem indicators	Several problem indicators	Clear direction	Healthy self-management

You Make Personal Choices and Decisions Daily

NEGATIVE, DESTRUCTIVE CHOICES	POSITIVE, CONSTRUCTIVE CHOICES
Emotionally Reactive: Let others control your emotions and behavior.	*Reflective & Proactive:* Self-manage your own emotions and behaviors.
OTHER DIRECTED	SELF-DIRECTED
REACTIVE ORIENTATION	INTELLIGENT SELF-DIRECTION

SELF-RENEWAL

Renewal is a self-directed process of positive personal change that brings your behavior in line with your important values. Research with professionals found that career achievement and satisfaction were positively related to EI-centric measures of Personal Excellence (Hammett, 2007). Intentionally working to develop your personal excellence and EI skills will help to stave off boredom and increase achievement and satisfaction. The relationship was demonstrated in the following ways:

- Personal Excellence was significantly related to satisfaction with meeting overall career goals.

- Personal Excellence was significantly related to satisfaction with career success.

- Personal Excellence was significantly related to satisfaction with meeting goals for income.

- Personal Excellence was significantly related to satisfaction with goals for developing career skills.

- Personal Excellence was significantly related to satisfaction with career for meeting one's existential needs, such as a deepening of spirituality.

- Personal Excellence was significantly related to satisfaction with career for meeting existential needs, such following one's true calling.

- Personal Excellence was significantly related to satisfaction with career for meeting existential needs, such as congruence and support of religious values.

When your behavior becomes too patterned, and you begin to feel bored and stuck, you may be arriving at a point in time for self-renewal. Most of us like to travel and experience new and novel places. This is a renewal experience resulting from physical change. Many people renew by direct contact with nature that lets them see, hear, and feel new experiences. A visit with a good friend or creating something tangible with your own hands may be renewing experiences. To see what *El Man* has to say about self-renewal, take a look at Exhibit 7.3.

Self-renewal is an emotional process that you can initiate to further develop your potential and increase the quality of your life. Follow the path illustrated in Exhibit 7.4 to begin your self-renewal process.

ACHIEVING ACADEMIC AND CAREER EXCELLENCE

A Personal Action Plan

Achieving excellence requires that you put into action what you have learned about the contributions of the emotional mind. We have encouraged you to think about and develop an emotionally healthy mind to improve your ability to achieve success and satisfaction. In our model, excellence is viewed as an intentional confluent learning process of creating opportunities through positive change and commitment to personal quality standards. Developing intentional habits that you use everyday enables you to achieve personal excellence in academics, career, and life.

EXHIBIT 7.3   *EI MAN* ON SELF-RENEWAL

Self-Renewal

Self-renewal is something that you do everyday to make yourself be a more complete, happier person.

You do this by using your emotional skills to behave wisely, think constructive thoughts and feel confident that you can "take care of business." If you act in a positive, friendly way, you model this to other people and many times it will "rub off" on them and it helps them to act in a similar way, which is beneficial to you and to them. In a sense, you are recycling yourself to become a better person, better able to deal effectively and constructively with the people and world around you. Believe it or not, this self-renewal will make you a younger person in your body, mind and spirit. It really works. The ancient Egyptians thought the sun died at night and was reborn at dawn. Today we know this isn't so, but there is no denying that, no matter how dark it gets at night, the next morning the sun is shining brightly, ready to go back to work.

> "IF THE SUN AND MOON SHOULD DOUBT, THEY'D IMMEDIATELY GO OUT!"
> —WILLIAM BLAKE
>
> BELIEVE IN YOURSELF, TRUST YOURSELF, & RENEW YOURSELF—EVERYDAY OF YOUR LIFE—JUST LIKE THE SUN.

You have completed the ESAP and gained valuable personal information and knowledge. You have worked through the Emotional Learning System and completed 13 emotional skill lessons. However, your plan should not be limited to one source. You can receive feedback, evaluative data, and responses from peers, supervisors, family, friends, coworkers, and other assessments. You also learn from your observations of people and the world around you. Use these important data and convert all the information into a personal action plan that you can use to achieve higher levels of excellence and satisfaction. As you develop your personal action plan, remember these important points:

- The emotional system is key to your health and success.
- Emotional intelligence is a learned ability requiring intentional, self-directed behaviors.
- Change is natural and occurs throughout life; managing change and transition requires self-knowledge, personal skills, and a positive attitude.
- High levels of achievement and success are self-defined and self-directed.

EXHIBIT 7.4	SYSTEMATIC SELF-RENEWAL

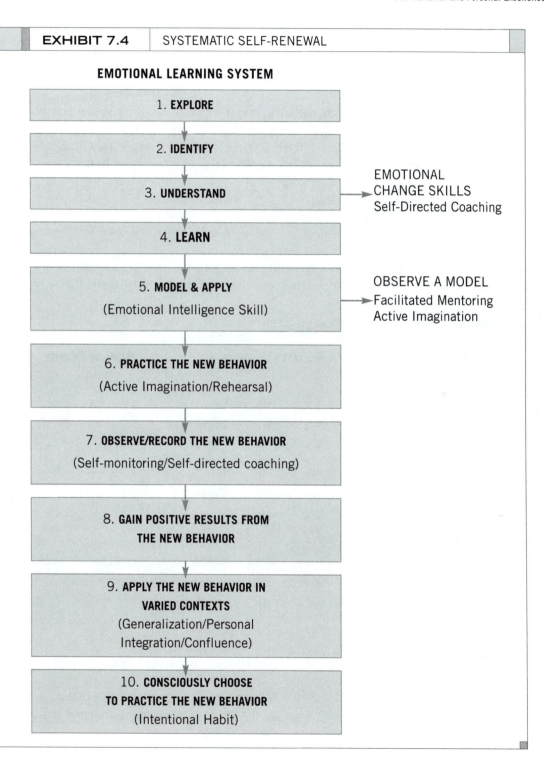

EMOTIONAL LEARNING SYSTEM

1. **EXPLORE**

2. **IDENTIFY**

3. **UNDERSTAND**

4. **LEARN**

5. **MODEL & APPLY**
(Emotional Intelligence Skill)

6. **PRACTICE THE NEW BEHAVIOR**
(Active Imagination/Rehearsal)

7. **OBSERVE/RECORD THE NEW BEHAVIOR**
(Self-monitoring/Self-directed coaching)

8. **GAIN POSITIVE RESULTS FROM**
THE NEW BEHAVIOR

9. **APPLY THE NEW BEHAVIOR IN**
VARIED CONTEXTS
(Generalization/Personal
Integration/Confluence)

10. **CONSCIOUSLY CHOOSE**
TO PRACTICE THE NEW BEHAVIOR
(Intentional Habit)

EMOTIONAL
CHANGE SKILLS
Self-Directed Coaching

OBSERVE A MODEL
Facilitated Mentoring
Active Imagination

- Relationships are important—build and manage relationships with skill, care, and respect.
- Emotional intelligence is the foundation for all learning, growth, and development.

Organize your ideas about the four major emotional intelligence competency areas: Interpersonal, Leadership, Self-Management, and Intrapersonal. Identify the order in which you wish to develop each competency and how each competency will help you achieve personal and career excellence.

1. _____
2. _____
3. _____
4. _____

Next, organize your ideas about the 13 emotional intelligence skills. Using Exhibit 7.5, identify the skills you wish to develop and rank them by

EXHIBIT 7.5   SKILL DEVELOPMENT

Emotional Skill	Requires Developing			Rank by Priority		
				A	B	C
Assertion	Yes	No	Maybe			
Anger Management	Yes	No	Maybe			
Anxiety Management	Yes	No	Maybe			
Social Awareness	Yes	No	Maybe			
Empathy	Yes	No	Maybe			
Decision Making	Yes	No	Maybe			
Positive Influence	Yes	No	Maybe			
Drive Strength	Yes	No	Maybe			
Commitment Ethic	Yes	No	Maybe			
Time Management	Yes	No	Maybe			
Positive Change	Yes	No	Maybe			
Self-Esteem	Yes	No	Maybe			
Stress Management	Yes	No	Maybe			

Why did you select particular skills? How will these skills help you achieve better results in your life? In your career? What are the benefits (the value to you) and the costs (the failure to develop) related to these 13 skills?

priority, using **A** for the most important, **B** for those second in importance, and **C** for those that are least important to you now.

The third step in completing your personal action plan is to prepare an extensive Personal Development Mission Statement and an extensive Career Development Mission Statement using the forms shown in Exhibits 7.6 and 7.7. Begin each statement by identifying two goals that you want to achieve.

EXHIBIT 7.6	PERSONAL DEVELOPMENT MISSION STATEMENT

Goal 1: _____
_____

Goal 2: _____
_____

My top-ranked emotional intelligence skills for personal development:
_____
_____
_____

Ideas and strategies for using *self-directed coaching* to achieve my personal goals:
_____
_____
_____

Ideas and strategies for using *emotional mentoring* to achieve my personal goals:
_____
_____
_____

Ideas and strategies for using *active imagination* to achieve my personal goals:
_____
_____
_____
_____

EXHIBIT 7.7	CAREER DEVELOPMENT MISSION STATEMENT

Goal 1:

Goal 2:

My top-ranked emotional intelligence skills for career development:

Ideas and strategies for using *self-directed coaching* to achieve my career goals:

Ideas and strategies for using *emotional mentoring* to achieve my career goals:

Ideas and strategies for using *active imagination* to achieve my career goals:

LIFELONG EMOTIONAL LEARNING

The majority of our time for the past 30 years has been spent helping people discover and use their potential for achieving happiness, success, and satisfaction in their careers, relationships, and personal lives. We have come to know that high levels of achievement, success, and happiness are self-defined and self-directed processes unique to each person. We have also come to believe that people have within themselves all that they need to live productive and satisfying lives. Our job has been to understand the process of positive personal change and to be helpful to people as they explore and develop emotional intelligence and build quality from within themselves.

THINGS TO REMEMBER

- Personal, academic, and career excellence is an individual, ongoing process that you have to define and direct. The process involves failures, learning, relearning, and personal changes.

- Becoming a person who likes and values Self, gets along well with others, and successfully meets the demands of daily life and work doesn't happen accidentally. You have to learn and practice skills.

- Developing emotional intelligence skills and wise behaviors brings mental and physical benefits.

- All people have strong points and weak points. Successful people know and acknowledge both their strengths and weaknesses.

- Problem behaviors that interfere with you reaching your goals need not define your future. Problem areas indicate where new skills are required.

- You cannot change your behavior unless you know specifically what to change and how to change it. Use and apply the Emotional Learning System daily.

- You have worth and value because you are a unique person. Base your self-worth on things about you that you can control—your behavior and integrity, for example—and not just on what you achieve.

- Asking for help from a skilled person that you respect and trust is a strength. Look for good models while learning the emotional intelligence skills. Ask skilled friends, coworkers, and others for help as you develop new behaviors.

What we must reach for is a conception of perpetual self-discovery, perpetual reshaping to realize one's best self, to be the person one could be.

JOHN GARDNER

LAST WORD

Thank you for exploring our model of emotional intelligence. We hope that you will apply the Emotional Learning System to improve your academic and career success and begin to focus on the positive contributions of the emotional mind.

IMAGINEERING ACTIVITIES FOR RENEWAL
AND DEVELOPMENT

ACTIVITY 7.1	IMAGINEERING YOUR BEST SELF

Personal/Professional Development Activity:
Imagineering Your Best Self

Name   Date

Current Position   Department/Unit

I. Personal Vision. What is your dream? Create a clear and vivid image of how you see yourself being when you are most successful and happy.

_____

II. Reflection. Review your self-assessment(s). Reflect and identify your specific strengths and areas that you want to develop in order to help you pursue your vision.

Current Strengths   Areas to Develop

_____   _____

_____   _____

_____   _____

III. Target. Focus now on your current strengths as behaviors to maintain and enhance. Select the one skill area to learn/develop that would be most important to you in helping you pursue your vision.

_____

IV. Action Plan. Where will you start? What specific behaviors will you engage and practice to develop your target skill? The behaviors you list will become your action plan for developing the emotional skills most important to you for reaching your vision.

_____

_____

_____

V. Personal Mission Statement. Write a personal mission statement based on what you have discovered.

_____

_____

ACTIVITY 7.2 | IMAGINEERING ORGANIZATIONAL EXCELLENCE

Leadership Development Activity:
Imagineering Organizational Excellence

Name   Date

Current Position   Department/Unit

I. Organizational Vision. What is the dream of your organization/institution? Write in your organization's vision. This is a team vision.

_____

II. Collaborative Development. What are the dreams of your followers, peers, and/or leaders? From the EI Leadership model, the role of the follower is to develop personal and organizational goal congruence, while the role of the leader is to collaborate with followers, constituents, and stake holders to develop and pursue both organizational vision and shared aspirations. Work with peers, followers, or leaders to create a clear and vivid image, a personal vision, of how they see themselves being when they are most successful and happy.

_____

III. Assessment. Use positive EI assessment(s) to explore and develop the individual and team.

IV. Reflection. Review the self-assessment(s). Reflect and identify specific and personally meaningful strengths and areas to develop in order to help pursue the personal vision.

Current Strengths   Areas to Develop

_____   _____

_____   _____

_____   _____

V. Target. Select the one skill area to learn/develop that would be most important to you in helping you pursue your vision.

_____

VI. Action Plan. What specific behaviors can be engaged and practiced to develop the target skill? The behaviors you list will become an action plan for developing the most important emotional skill.

_____

_____

_____

VII. Capture Shared Aspirations. Combine the organizational and personal visions you have created with targeted skills and identified behaviors needed for personally meaningful development. What could you and the organization do collaboratively that would help you pursue both visions?

_____

Emotional Intelligence Theories

EMOTIONAL INTELLIGENCE THEORIES

In this section, several theories of emotional intelligence are presented and compared to either the Emotional Skills Assessment Process (ASAP) or the Emotional Learning System. Our model is only one of many, and we encourage you to explore the ideas and thoughts expressed by other approaches.

Peter Salovey and John Mayer (1990) developed a model of emotional intelligence and defined five domains of emotional intelligence as:

1. *Self-Awareness:* observing yourself and recognizing a feeling as it happens.
2. *Managing Emotions:* handling feelings in an appropriate manner; realizing the reasons for a particular feeling; and finding ways to deal with fear, anxiety, anger, and sadness.
3. *Motivating Self:* channeling emotions in the service of a goal, possessing emotional self-control, delaying gratification, and stifling impulses.
4. *Empathy:* expressing sensitivity to others' feelings and concerns and understanding their perspective; appreciating the different ways that people feel about things.
5. *Handling Relationships:* dealing with others' emotions, social competence, and social skills.

A key to understanding emotional learning and emotional intelligence is to personally understand and feel what is involved in the Salovey–Mayer model. It is relatively easy to understand the five domains and the central concepts of each; however, it is also necessary to feel the difference between emotional intelligence content and its actual use and expression in your daily life. It is

EXHIBIT A.1	INTEGRATING THE ESAP AND THE FIVE DOMAINS OF EMOTIONAL INTELLIGENCE

Five Domains of Emotional Intelligence	Emotional Skills Assessment Process
1. Self-Awareness	The actual process of assessing emotional skills; includes self-monitoring
2. Managing Emotions	Involves the stress management, assertion, anger management, anxiety management, empathy, social awareness, and positive change emotional skills
3. Motivating Self	Involves the drive strength, decision making, time management, commitment ethic, positive influence, self-esteem, and positive change emotional skills
4. Empathy	Involves the empathy, social awareness, self-esteem, assertion, and positive influence emotional skills
5. Handling Relationships	Involves the self-esteem, empathy, assertion, stress management, anger management, anxiety management, positive influence, and positive change emotional skills

essential to personally relate to how emotional learning and knowledge is a vital construct of intelligence and a learned human ability.

Exhibit A.1, Integrating the ESAP and the Five Domains of Emotional Intelligence, illustrates how specific emotional skills are used to understand and develop, on a practical level, each of the five domains.

Howard Gardner (1983, 1993), who developed the Multiple Intelligences Theory, has emphasized the importance of the Interpersonal and Intrapersonal intelligences. He defined *interpersonal intelligence* as the ability to understand others and *intrapersonal intelligence* as the capacity to form an accurate veridical model of oneself and to use that model to operate effectively in life. Gardner has worked with others to continue the research into and development of the Multiple Intelligences Theory. As a result, *intelligence* is defined as the ability to solve problems or to make things that are valued by a culture. Gardner and other pioneers in emotional intelligence are creating new ways of viewing individual development, creativity, and leadership (Gardner, Mayer, & Sternberg, 1997).

Daniel Goleman has written several best-selling books about emotional intelligence and its importance in education and business. In *Emotional Intelligence: Why It Can Matter More Than IQ for Character, Health, and Lifelong Achievement* (1995), he stated that, in the years to come, the skills that help people harmonize will become increasingly valued as a workplace asset. In

EXHIBIT A.2	EMOTIONAL COMPETENCE FRAMEWORK AND ESAP

Emotional Competence Framework	Emotional Skills Assessment Process
Personal Competence (how we manage emotions)	Learnable emotional skills
1. Self-Awareness: knowing one's internal states, preferences, resources, and intuitions	The actual process of exploring and developing emotional skills and competencies
2. Self-Regulation: managing one's internal states, impulses, and resources	Involves the assertion, anger management, anxiety management, self-esteem, stress management, and positive change skills
3. Motivation: emotional tendencies that guide or help us to reach goals	Involves Performance Area III: Self-Management and includes the positive influence, drive strength, time management, self-esteem, and commitment ethic skills
4. Empathy: an awareness of others' feelings, needs, and concerns	Involves Performance Area I: Interpersonal Skills, and Performance Area II: Leadership Skills, and includes the assertion, empathy, social awareness, decision making, and positive influence skills
5. Social Skills: an adeptness at inducing desirable responses from others	Involves the positive influence, empathy, social awareness, anger management, anxiety management, stress management, assertion, self-esteem, and positive change skills

Working with Emotional Intelligence (1998), Goleman affirmed the value of emotional intelligence and illustrated how it is critical to the performance of people and organizations. He presented numerous, compelling examples of why and how emotional intelligence is more valuable than the traditional views of IQ. Goleman described the Emotional Competence Framework model that is organized around personal and social competencies. Exhibit A.2 compares the personal competence portion of Goleman's Emotional Competence Framework to the ESAP model—on a practical level, this comparison illustrates how specific skills can be learned to develop emotional intelligence.

Robert Sternberg (1985, 1995) cited examples, grounded in his research and experience, that support the view that intelligence is an ability to adapt to new surroundings and solve problems. He noted that successful people exhibit practical intelligence that may be a better predictor of success than traditional types of intelligence tests. His studies supported the view that nontraditional intelligence is certainly more practical, as well as a stronger, predictor of human performance.

Hendrie Weisenger (1985, 1998) documented and illustrated the effect of emotions in personal and work settings. He defined emotional intelligence as the intelligent use of emotions. He emphasized the importance of intentionally learning and making emotions work to enhance results both intrapersonally (helping Self) and interpersonally (helping others). Weisenger provided many examples that show how emotional intelligence can be developed and nurtured by learning and practicing particular skills: Self-Awareness, Emotional Management, and Self-Motivation.

Robert Cooper and Ayman Sawaf (1997) provided evidence and extensive experience that supported the value and necessity of emotional intelligence in developing leadership and successful organizations. In *Executive EQ: Emotional Intelligence in Leadership and Organizations*, emotional intelligence is defined as the ability to sense, understand, and effectively apply the power and acumen of emotion as a source of human energy, information, connection, and influence. In their model, the four cornerstones of emotional intelligence are Emotional Literacy, Emotional Fitness, Emotional Depth, and Emotional Alchemy.

Pat Townsend and Joan Gebhardt (1997) pointed to the critical importance of emotional intelligence skills for effective leadership. In *Five Star Leadership*, they presented a value analysis diagram for practicing effective leadership. Emotional intelligence skills are at the heart of each of their value diagrams: Knowing Self, Influencing Others, and Accomplishing Tasks.

As a result of studies conducted at the UCLA Higher Education Research Institute, A.W. Astin and H. Astin (1993) concluded that leadership is a proactive, collective, cooperative, and collaborative effort. (Their seven Cs of leadership include many of the skills and competencies of emotional intelligence.)

Current research from many sources supports the value and importance of emotional learning and emotional intelligence. Achieving excellence in work and life depends on the positive contributions of the emotional system. By its very nature, emotional intelligence is highly personal and unique to each person. Personal meaning is stronger for most people than external meaning derived from data, content, and information. When you learn to personally relate to the concept of emotional intelligence, understand the emotional system, and clearly identify its skills and competencies, you make an important discovery. When you learn to use and fully develop emotional intelligence, you have gained the most important set of skills and competencies for your success and health throughout life.

The development of emotional intelligence is a dynamic and fluid learning process rich with personal meaning. The ESAP is a discovery and learning model that enables you to gain emotional information and knowledge about

EXHIBIT A.3	EMOTIONAL SKILLS RELATED TO THE HABITS OF HIGHLY EFFECTIVE PEOPLE

Habits	Emotional Skills Assessment Process
1. Personal Vision (be proactive)	The process of exploring and developing emotional intelligence skills.
2. Personal Leadership (begin with the end in mind)	The process of learning and improving emotional intelligence skills. Understanding and using the emotional system. Involves the Leadership competency area.
3. Personal Management (put first things first)	The process of learning and improving emotional intelligence skills. Involves the Self-Management competency area, including the time management, drive strength, commitment ethic, and positive change emotional intelligence skills.
4. Interpersonal Leadership (think win–win)	Involves the Interpersonal and Leadership competency areas, including the assertion, empathy, social awareness, positive influence, and decision-making emotional intelligence skills.
5. Empathic Communication (seek first to understand, then to be understood)	Involves the Interpersonal, Leadership, and Intrapersonal competency areas, including the empathy, social awareness, positive influence, assertion, anger management, anxiety management, stress management, and self-esteem emotional intelligence skills.
6. Creative Cooperation (synergize)	The process of exploring and developing all 13 emotional intelligence skills.
7. Renewal (sharpen the saw)	The process of exploring and developing all 13 emotional intelligence skills.

you. Then, you can use this new information and knowledge to develop emotional health and achieve excellence.

A landmark model of human performance underscores the importance of emotional intelligence to overall effectiveness and healthy adjustments to life. Stephen Covey's *The 7 Habits of Highly Effective People: Powerful Lessons in Personal Change* (1989) provides a blueprint for effectiveness in work and life. Exhibit A.3 illustrates the relationship between the ESAP and Covey's model.

We believe that emotional intelligence competency areas and skills are key to personal effectiveness in all aspects of life and work.

EXHIBIT A.4	ERIKSON'S STAGES OF DEVELOPMENT AND THE ESAP

Stages	Emotional Skills Assessment Process
1. Infancy: Trust vs. Mistrust	Importance of learning emotional safety and security early in life. Emotional system is key. Learning and improving emotional intelligence skills begins early in life.
2. Early Childhood: Autonomy vs. Shame, Doubt	Intrapersonal growth and development, including the self-esteem skill. Learning the foundation of all areas of emotional intelligence.
3. Play Age: Initiative vs. Guilt	Involves the Interpersonal and Intrapersonal competency areas, including the anger management, anxiety management, self-esteem, and stress management skills.
4. School Age: Industry vs. Inferiority	Involves the Interpersonal, Intrapersonal, and Self-Management competency areas, including the drive strength, time management, and commitment ethic skills.
5. Adolescence: Identity Confusion	Involves developing the self-esteem, assertion, empathy, social awareness, positive influence, decision-making, anger management, anxiety management, and stress management skills.
6. Young Adult: Intimacy vs. Isolation	Involves developing the assertion, empathy, social awareness, anger management, anxiety management, stress management, and positive change skills.
7. Adulthood: Generativity vs. Stagnation	The process of understanding and using emotional intelligence skills to increase productivity and satisfaction. Using the emotional system to renew Self and achieve excellence.
8. Mature Age: Integrity vs. Despair	Continuing to develop emotional intelligence skills to maintain productivity, emotional health, personal renewal, and a positive approach to life stress and change.

Another landmark model of human growth and development is Erik Erikson's (1968) Stages of Psychosocial Development over a lifetime. Exhibit A.4 compares the ESAP to the Erikson's stages of development.

At each of the psychosocial stages of development and as people move fluidly back and forth throughout life, the emotional system is the key element of the human condition. An understanding of the emotional system helps people successfully meet the demands and challenges of each stage of life. Emotional intelligence skills enable people to reduce negative stress in their life, build healthy relationships, communicate effectively, and develop emotional health. Emotional safety is important at each stage of development. These same skills and competencies are critical to achieving excellence in life and work.

As people explore new ways to understand the emotional system and emotional intelligence, they discover that self-awareness is the key to making positive personal changes. An honest and positive assessment is at the heart of personal growth, development, and change. Before most people are willing to change, they should know which behaviors to keep and which behaviors to change and develop. Self-exploration is critical to the type of awareness necessary for positive and intentional personal change.

REFERENCES

Astin, A. W. & Astin, H. (1993). *A social change model of leadership development: Guidebook version III.* College Park, MD: National Clearinghouse for Leadership Programs.

Astin, A. W., Gardner, J. N., & Sax, L. J. (1998). *The changing American college student: Implications for the freshman year and beyond.* Columbia, SC: A special satellite conference on the First-Year Experience presented by the University of South Carolina.

Babior, S. & Goldman, C. (1996). *Overcoming panic anxiety & phobias: New strategies to free yourself from worry and fear.* Duluth, MN: Pfeifer-Hamilton.

Bennett, M. E. (1933). *College and life.* New York: McGraw-Hill.

Bickel, R. D. & Lake, P. F. (1994). Reconceptualizing the university's duty to provide a safe learning environment: A criticism of the doctrine of in loco parentis and the restatement (second) of torts. *Journal of College and University Law, 20,* 261–293.

Bloland, P. A., Stamatakos, L. C., & Rogers, R. R. (1994). *Reform in student affairs: A critique of student development.* Greensboro, NC: ERIC Clearinghouse on Counseling & Student Services.

Cooper, R. K. & Sawaf, A. (1997). *Executive EQ: Emotional intelligence in leadership and organizations.* New York: Putnam.

Covey, S. R. (1989). *The 7 Habits of highly effective people: Powerful lessons in personal change.* New York: Simon & Schuster.

Cox, J. E. & Nelson, D. B. (2008). Quantifying emotional intelligence: The relationship between thinking patterns and emotional skills. *Humanistic Counseling, Education and Development, 47*(1), 9–25.

Damasio, A. R. (1994). *Descartes' error: Emotion, reason, and the human brain.* New York: Avon Books.

Davenport, E., Nelson, D. B., & Low, G. R. (2000). *The Effect of Teacher Mentors on the Academic Excellence of Preservice Teachers—The Texas A&M, Kingsville Experience.* Paper presented at the annual conference of the International Mentoring Association, New Orleans, LA.

Dryden, G. & Vos, J. (1994). *The learning revolution.* Winnipeg, Canada: Skills of Learning Publications.

Eberhard, J., Reinhardt-Mondragon, P., & Stottlemyer, B. (2000). *Strategies for new teacher retention: Creating a climate of authentic professional development for teachers with three or less years of experience.* Paper presented at the South Texas Research and Development Center at Texas A&M University, Corpus Christi.

Epstein, S. (1998). *Constructive thinking: The key to emotional intelligence.* Westport, CT: Praeger.

Erikson, E. H. (1968). *Identity: Youth and crisis.* New York: Norton.

Etzioni, A. (1961). *A comparative analysis of complex organizations.* New York: The Free Press.

Ferrett, S. K. (1994). *Peak performance.* Burr Ridge, IL: Irwin Mirror Press.

Gardner, H. (1983). *Frames of mind.* New York: Basic Books.

Gardner, H. (1993). *Multiple intelligences: The theory in practice.* New York: Basic Books.

Gardner, H., Mayer, J., & Sternberg, R. (1997). *Expanding our concept of intelligence.* Paper presented at the annual meeting of the American Educational Research Association, Chicago, IL.

Gardner, J. N. (1998). *The freshman seminar and the first-year experience: Student success and retention.* Columbia, SC: A special satellite conference on the First-Year Experience presented by the University of South Carolina.

Gardner, J. W. (1963). *Excellence: Can we be equal and excellent too?* New York: Harper & Row.

Goleman, D. (1995). *Emotional intelligence: Why it can matter more than IQ for character, health, and lifelong achievement.* New York: Bantam Books.

Goleman, D. (1998). *Working with emotional intelligence.* New York: Bantam Books.

Greenspan, S. I. (1997). *The growth of the mind: And the endangered origins of intelligence.* New York: Addison-Wesley.

Hammett, R. D. (2007). *Personal Excellence Map (PEM) intervention and interpretation guide.* Corpus Christi, TX: Emotional Intelligence Learning Systems, Inc.

Hersey, P. & Blanchard, K. H. (1988). *Management of organizational behavior: Utilizing human resources.* Englewood Cliffs, NJ: Prentice Hall.

Ilardo, J. (1992). *Risk-taking for personal growth.* Oakland, CA: New Harbinger Publications.

Justice, M. & Espinosa, S. (2007). Emotional intelligence and beginning teacher candidates. *Education 127*(4), 456–461.

Kohn, A. (2000). *The case against standardized testing: Raising the scores; ruining the schools.* Westport, CT: Heinemann Press.

Komives, S. R. & Woodard, D. B. Jr. (Eds.). (1996). *Student services: A handbook for the profession* (3rd ed.). San Francisco: Jossey-Bass.

Kouzes, J. M. & Posner, B. Z. (1999). *Encouraging the heart: A leader's guide to rewarding and recognizing others.* San Francisco: Jossey-Bass.

Kouzes, J. M. & Posner, B. Z. (1999). *The leadership challenge.* San Francisco: Jossey-Bass.

Low, G. R. (1997). *Dimensions of the modern superintendency: Assessing personal, relationship, and emotional skills.* Paper presented at the annual meeting of the Southern Regional Council on Educational Administration, Charleston, SC.

Low, G. R. (1998). *The missing dimension of educational leadership: Emotional intelligence: A model for broad-range leadership development.* Paper presented at the annual meeting of the Southern Regional Council on Educational Administration, Savannah, GA.

Low, G. R. (2000). *Emotional intelligence: A positive model for personal and career excellence.* Paper presented at the South Texas Women's Conference, Texas A&M University, Kingsville.

Low, G. R. & Nelson, D. B. (1999). *Building healthy students, schools, and communities: Achieving excellence in education through emotional intelligence.* San Antonio, TX: Texas Education Agency, Texas A&M University System and Sid W. Richardson Foundation.

Low, G. R. & Nelson, D. B. (1999). *Emotional intelligence: The key to achievement, retention, career excellence, and leadership.* Paper presented at the annual meeting of the Texas Association of College and University Student Personnel Administrators, South Padre Island, TX.

Low, G. R. & Nelson, D. B. (2000). *Achieving excellence in education through emotional intelligence.* Paper presented at the annual conference of the Texas Association of Future Educators, San Antonio, TX.

Low, G. R. & Nelson, D. B. (2000). *Emotional intelligence: Essential skills for academic and career success: A research-based learner-centered model for teachers, children, and adolescents.* Paper presented at the Fifth Annual National Coalition for At-Risk Children & Youth, Texas Women's University, Denton, TX.

Low, G. R. & Nelson, D. B. (2000). *Quantifying emotional intelligence: Positive contributions of the emotional mind.* Dr. Low's Keynote Address and Invited Paper for the Spring 2000 Faculty Lecture at Texas A&M University, Kingsville.

Low, G. R. & Nelson D. B. (Spring 2004). Emotional intelligence: Effectively bridging the gap between high school and college. *Texas Study of Secondary Education* XIII(2), 7–10.

Low, G. R. & Nelson D. B. (Spring 2005). Emotional intelligence: The role of transformational learning in academic excellence. *Texas Study of Secondary Education* XIV(2), 41–44.

Low, G. R., Nelson, D. B., & Litton, F. (2000). *Positive leadership and emotional stress management: A professional development and renewal workshop for superintendents.* Kingsville, TX: A program conducted for superintendents in South Texas at Texas A&M University, Kingsville.

Low, G. R., Nelson, D. B., Stottlemyer, B., & Davenport, E. (2000). *Exploring and developing emotionally intelligent teachers.* Paper presented at the Fourth Annual Conference on School–University Partnerships, convened by the Texas A&M University System and the Texas Education Agency, Austin, TX.

Low, G. R., Nelson, D. B., & Supley, M. (1998). *Exploring and developing emotional intelligence: An adult learning model.* Paper presented at the annual conference of the Commission on Adult and Basic Education, Corpus Christi, TX.

Low, G. R., Nelson, D. B., & Supley, M. (1999). *Emotional intelligence and personal leadership: Essential elements of successful 21st century learning communities.* Paper presented at the Galaxy II Leadership Summit and the American Association of Adult and Continuing Education, San Antonio, TX.

McGregor, D. (1960). *The human side of enterprise.* New York: McGraw-Hill.

McKay, M., Davis, M., & Eshleman, E. (1987). *The relaxation and stress reduction workbook.* Oakland, CA: New Harbinger Publications.

McKay, M., Davis, M., & Fanning, P. (1981). *Thoughts and feelings: The art of cognitive stress intervention.* Oakland, CA: New Harbinger Publications.

McKay, M. & Fanning, P. (1987). *Self-esteem: A proven program of cognitive techniques for assessing, improving, and maintaining your self-esteem.* Oakland, CA: New Harbinger Publications.

McKay, M. & Fanning, P. (1997). *Prisoners of belief: Exposing & changing beliefs that control your life.* Oakland, CA: New Harbinger Publications.

McQuary, J. P. (1983). *Personal skills development in an educational setting.* Paper presented at the Personal Skills Mapping Conference, Corpus Christi, TX.

Nelson, D. B. (2008). Personal excellence: A new paradigm for gifted education. In Y. Freeman, D. Freeman, & R. Ramirez (Eds.), *Diverse learners in the mainstream classroom* (chapter 5, 101–117). Portsmouth, HN: Heinemann.

Nelson, D. B. (2009). *AWAKE emotional intelligence journal.* Corpus Christi, TX: Emotional Intelligence Learning Systems, Inc.

Nelson, D. B. & Low, G. R. (1980). *Achievement, retention, and counseling intervention strategies for migrant students.* Austin, TX: An applied research study and publication of Education Service Center, Region 2 and Texas Education Agency.

Nelson, D. B. & Low, G. R. (1993). *Personal skills mapping.* Oakland, CA: Margo Murray-Hicks and Associates.

Nelson, D. B. & Low, G. R. (1998). *Exploring and developing intelligence skills.* Corpus Christi, TX: Emotional Learning Systems.

Nelson, D. B. & Low, G. R. (1999). *Achieving excellence through emotional intelligence.* Corpus Christi, TX and Kingsville, TX: Professional development workshops for educators, human resource professionals, counselors, and managers at Texas A&M University–Corpus Christi and Texas A&M University, Kingsville.

Nelson, D. B. & Low, G. R. (1999). *Learning and improving emotional intelligence skills.* Corpus Christi, TX: Emotional Learning Systems.

Nelson, D. B. & Low, G. R. (1999). *The Success Profiler*™. Oshkosh, WI: The Conover Company.

Nelson, D. B. & Low, G. R. (2000). *Emotional intelligence: A positive assessment and student-centered learning model.* Houston: A Pre-Conference Professional Development Workshop presented for the annual conference of the Texas Counseling Association.

Nelson, D. B. & Low, G. R. (2000). *Emotional intelligence: Key factors in personal, academic, and career excellence.* Paper presented at the annual conference of the First-Year Experience, University of South Carolina, Columbia.

Nelson, D. B. & Low, G. R. (2007). Emotional intelligence and college success: A research-based assessment and intervention model. In J. Cassidy, A. Martinez, & C. Swift (Eds.), *Supporting student success* (chapter 17, 236–247). Corpus Christi, TX: Texas A&M University-Corpus Christi.

Nelson, D. B. & Low, G. R. (Fall 2008). Helping at-risk adolescents succeed: An EI centric model. *Texas Study of Secondary Education XVII*(2), 11–13.

Nelson, D., Low, G., & Davenport, E. (2000). *Improving emotional intelligence skills: A professional development model for mentor teacher and protégés.* Paper presented at the annual conference of the International Mentoring Association, New Orleans, LA.

Nelson, D. B., Low, G. R., & Ellis, R. F. (2007). Emotional intelligence: A transformative theory and applied model of positive personal change. *Annals of the American Psychotherapy Association, 10*(4), 30–35.

Nelson, D. B., Low, G. R., Hammett, R. D. & Sen, A. (2009). *Emotional intelligence coaching map.* Corpus Christi, TX: Emotional Intelligence Learning Systems, Inc.

Nelson, D. B. & Nelson, K. (1999). *Emotional intelligence skills: Significant factors in freshmen achievement and retention.* Paper presented at the conference on the First-Year Experience, University of South Carolina, Columbia.

Oakley-Browne, H. (1998, August). *MMHA mentor newsletter.* Oakland, CA: Margo Murray-Hicks and Associates.

Pelletier, K. (1977). *Mind as healer, mind as slayer: A holistic approach to preventive stress disorders.* New York: Dell.

Perkins, D. (1995). *Outsmarting IQ: The emerging science of learnable intelligence.* New York: The Free Press.

Richardson, Sid W. Foundation. (1990–1995). *The professional development school: A commonsense approach to improving education; principals for schools in Texas, and restructuring the university reward system.* Fort Worth, TX: Reports on Education in Texas.

Richardson, Sid W. Foundation. (1998–1999). The Richardson Fellow program. Fort Worth, TX: Texas A&M University System conferences for Richardson Fellows.

Rosen, R. & Berger, L. (1991). *The healthy company: Eight strategies to develop people, productivity, and profits.* New York: Putnam.

Salovey, P. & Mayer, J. D. (1990). *Emotional intelligence: Imagination, cognition, and personality.* New York: Harper.

Scott, G. G. (1990). *Resolving conflict: With others and with yourself.* Oakland, CA: New Harbinger Publications.

Seligman, M. E. (1990). *Learned optimism.* New York: Alfred A. Knopf.

Selye, H. (1980). *The stress of life.* New York: McGraw-Hill.

Sen, A., Nelson, D., & Rao, S. (2009). *Fuelling success: How emotional intelligence helped HPCL and its employees to grow.* Mumbai, India: Book World Enterprises.

Senge, P. M. (1990). *The fifth dimension: The art & practice of the learning organization.* New York: Doubleday.

Sternberg, R. J. (1985). *Beyond IQ: A triarchic theory of human intelligence.* Cambridge: Cambridge University Press.

Sternberg, R. J. (1995). *Successful intelligence: How practical and creative intelligence determine success in life.* New York: Simon & Schuster.

Sternberg, R. J. & Davidson, J. E. (Eds.). (1990). Intelligence testing. *Educational Psychologist, 25*(3/4) Special issue.

Stevenson, L. & Burger, M. (1989). *Characteristics of at-risk youth.* Austin, TX: Texas Education Agency and Drop-out Information Clearinghouse.

Supley, M. (1998). *Preparing leaders today for tomorrow: Assessing and building skills in the missing dimension of educational leadership: Emotional intelligence.* Paper presented at the annual meeting of the Southern Regional Council on Educational Administration, Savannah, GA.

Supley, M. (1999). *Character qualities of quality administrators: A consideration of personal character qualities.* Juried paper presented at the Educational Leadership and Law Conference, Atlanta, GA.

Supley, M. & Low, G. R. (1998). *Beginning now....* Corpus Christi, TX: Emotional Learning Systems.

Supley, M. & Low, G. R. (1999). *Administration, leadership, and emotional intelligence: An essential component for successful outcomes.* Paper presented at the Educational Leadership and Law Conference, Atlanta, GA.

Tarvis, C. (1999). *Anger: The misunderstood emotion.* New York: Simon & Schuster.

Texas Education Agency. (1995). *Learner-centered proficiencies for teachers, administrators, and counselors in Texas.* Austin, TX: Author.

Townsend, P. & Gebhardt, J. (1997). *Five star leadership.* New York: Wiley.

Weber, M. (1947). *The theory of social and economic organization* (A. M. Henderson & T. Parsons, Trans. & Eds.). New York: The Free Press.

Weisenger, H. (1985). *Dr. Weisenger's anger work-out book.* New York: Quill Press.

Weisenger, H. (1998). *Emotional intelligence at work.* San Francisco: Jossey-Bass.

RELATED DOCTORAL DISSERTATIONS

Abney, B. C. (1984). *The effects of behavior-control-perception (BCP) training upon select graduate students emphasizing business management or human resources development.* Unpublished doctoral dissertation, East Texas State University, Commerce.

Bradshaw, S. (1981). *PSM scale differences of successful and unsuccessful CETA training.* Unpublished doctoral dissertation, John Wood College, Quincy, IL.

Branaman, T. (1981). *Multiple correlational analysis of quantity and frequency of alcohol use, problem drinking and personal life skills by ninth and twelfth grade students.* Unpublished doctoral dissertation, East Texas State University, Commerce.

Castro, V. (2005). The efficacy of an emotional intelligence based program: Resilient behaviors of seventh and eighth grade students. *Dissertation Abstracts International 66* (5). (UMI NO. 3175019)

Ceasar, P. (1989). *A comparison of personal skills of select psychologically "androgynous" and "masculine" males during mid-life.* Unpublished doctoral dissertation, East Texas State University, Commerce.

Chao, C. T. (2003). *Foreign language anxiety and emotional intelligence: A study of EFL students in Taiwan.* Unpublished doctoral dissertation, Texas A&M University–Kingsville.

Cox, J. E. (2010). *Quantifying emotional intelligence in relationships: The validation of the relationship skills map (RSM).* Unpublished doctoral dissertation, Texas A&M University-Kingsville.

Deatley, M. (1986). *The effects of interpersonal skills training (1PST) upon communication, discrimination, interpersonal, and leadership skills in business.* Unpublished doctoral dissertation, East Texas State University, Commerce.

Ellis, C. N. (2004). A study of emotional intelligence indicators in continuation and comprehensive high school students. *Dissertation Abstract International, 65* (8). (UMI NO. 3142248)

Farnia, F. (2007). *The relationship between emotional intelligence skills and foreign language proficiency.* Unpublished thesis, Allameh Tabatabaei University, Tehran, Iran.

Fernandez, A. (2007). *Attitudinal, behavioral, and emotional intelligence skill characteristics of college student-parents.* Unpublished doctoral dissertation, Texas A&M University–Kingsville.

Fry, L. (1990). *An evaluation of Mississippi State University's summer scholar's program.* Unpublished doctoral dissertation, Mississippi State University, Mississippi State.

Hale, K. D. (1986). *The effects of behavior-control-perception (BCP) training upon focus-of-control and personal skills of selected high-risk community college students.* Unpublished doctoral dissertation, East Texas State University, Commerce.

Hammett, R. (2007). *Personal excellence: The development and validation of a new measure of emotional intelligence.* Unpublished doctoral dissertation, Texas A&M University– Kingsville.

Hwang, F.-F. (2007). *The relationship between emotional intelligence and teaching effectiveness.* Unpublished doctoral dissertation, Texas A&M University–Kingsville.

Jagers, J. L. (1987). *Interpersonal and intrapersonal attributes of never-married singles.* Unpublished doctoral dissertation, University of North Texas, Denton.

Josefowitz, A. J. (1984). *The effects of management development training on organizational climate.* Unpublished doctoral dissertation, University of Minnesota, St. Paul.

Kostock, A. (1981). *An analysis of personal skills and clinical performance evaluation of associate degree nursing students.* Unpublished doctoral dissertation, University of Texas at Austin.

Leaseburg, M. G. (1990). *Validity and reliability study of an instrument for identifying educationally at-risk junior high school students.* Unpublished doctoral dissertation, Oklahoma State University, Stillwater.

Liang, Y. H. (2007). *The relationship between personality type and emotional intelligence in a sample of college and university faculty in Taiwan.* Unpublished doctoral dissertation, Texas A&M University–Kingsville.

Link, S. W. (1982). *Factors associated with academic performance of community college students.* Unpublished doctoral dissertation, University of North Texas, Denton.

Lu, S.-C. (2008). *Validation of a measure of emotional intelligence for first year college students in a Hispanic serving institution.* Unpublished doctoral dissertation, Texas A&M University–Kingsville.

Martinez, M. R. (2007). *An evaluation study of a college success course as a counseling intervention at a South Texas institution of higher education.* Unpublished doctoral dissertation, Texas A&M University–Kingsville.

Mead, A. M. (1985). *The ABC program and its impact on Columbus, Ohio students: A follow-up study for the compensatory, minority education, academically talented, scholarship programs.* Unpublished doctoral dissertation, Ohio State University, Columbus.

Millan, R. O. (2008). *Examining emotional intelligence differences among nursing students at a college in South Texas.* Unpublished doctoral dissertation, Texas A&M University-Kingsville.

Nelson, K. (1981). *A comparison of levels of personal skills in distressed and non-distressed marriages.* Unpublished doctoral dissertation, East Texas State University, Commerce.

Pope, P. (1981). *The relationship of selected intrapersonal, interpersonal, and life management skills to academic achievement among secondary school students.* Unpublished doctoral dissertation, East Texas State University, Commerce.

Potter, G. (2005). *The impact of an emotional intelligence intervention program on freshman students at a South Texas higher education institution.* Unpublished doctoral dissertation, Texas A&M University–Kingsville.

Quintanilla, M. C. (1998). *The effects of a stress intervention strategy in residential treatment staff: The PACE program.* Unpublished doctoral dissertation, St. Mary's University, San Antonio, TX.

Reyes-Dominguez, P. (2008). *The relationship between emotional intelligence and leadership on organizational excellence.* Unpublished doctoral dissertation, Texas A&M University–Kingsville.

Rice, D. M. (2006). An examination of emotional intelligence: Its relationship to academic achievement in army JROTC and the implications for education. *Dissertation Abstracts International.* (UMI NO. 3240023)

Saenz, T. (2009). *An exploratory study of the relationship between emotional intelligence and IQ: Implications for students with learning disabilities.* Unpublished doctoral dissertation, Texas A&M University–Kingsville.

Smith, B. (1983). *A comparison of trained and non-trained academically deficient students taught by peer counselors using the microcounseling model in an urban university.* Unpublished doctoral dissertation, Texas Southern University, Houston.

Smith, M. E. (2004). A mixed paradigm: Study of a transformational learning program for at-risk high school students. *Dissertation Abstract International,* 65 (11). (UMI No. 3152489)

Solis, V. R. (2007). *A comparison of personal inventories between speakers of two languages.* Unpublished doctoral dissertation, Texas A&M University–Kingsville.

Stottlemyer, B. G. (2002). *A conceptual framework for emotional intelligence in education: Factors affecting student achievement.* Unpublished doctoral dissertation, Texas A&M University–Kingsville.

Suudimenlakki, P. (1985). *A study of Finnish and American managers.* Unpublished doctoral dissertation, University of Helsinki, Helsinki, Finland.

Tang, H.-W. (2007). *A cross-cultural investigation of academic leaders' emotional intelligence and leadership effectiveness in Taiwan and the United States.* Unpublished doctoral dissertation, Texas A&M University–Kingsville.

Teliz Triujeque, R. (2009). *Validation of the Spanish version of the emotional skills assessment process (ESAP) with college students in Mexico.* Unpublished doctoral dissertation, Texas A&M University–Kingsville.

Tennant, S. (1990). *Personal and moral development curriculum intervention for liberal arts freshmen: A personal development program.* Unpublished doctoral dissertation, Ohio State University, Columbus.

Titus, J. (1980). *The effects of a human communications workshop on the self-actualization and interpersonal skills of United States Air Force and Civil Service personnel.* Unpublished doctoral dissertation, Abilene Christian University, Abilene, TX.

Turnquist, R. (1980). *Assessing the personal skills development of incarcerated juvenile delinquents.* Unpublished doctoral dissertation, Sam Houston State University, Huntsville, TX.

Vela, R. H., Jr. (2003). *The role of emotional intelligence in the academic achievement of first year college students.* Unpublished doctoral dissertation, Texas A&M University–Kingsville.

Walker, M. (1982). *Relationships among family of origin, personal skills, and selected interpersonal facilitative skills.* Unpublished doctoral dissertation, East Texas State University, Commerce.

Webb, J. (1991). *Patterns of social skills in a typology of marital systems.* Unpublished doctoral dissertation, The Fielding Institute, Santa Barbara, CA.

Welsh, S. (1985). *Can the academic probation student be salvaged? A retention strategy.* Unpublished doctoral dissertation, Kansas State University, Manhattan.

White, F. (1981). *Affective vocabulary and personal adjustment of deaf and hearing adolescent populations.* Unpublished doctoral dissertation, East Texas State University, Commerce.

Wilkins, D. D. (2004). *The relationship between emotional intelligence and enrollment retention in online instruction.* Unpublished doctoral dissertation, Walden University, Minneapolis, MN.

Williams, M. H. (2004). *Achievement and retention patterns in a predominantly Hispanic serving institution of higher education.* Unpublished doctoral dissertation, Texas A&M University–Kingsville.

Yin, M.-C. (2007). *Grey system theory and multiple attribute decision making: An innovative approach to educational research.* Unpublished doctoral dissertation, Texas A&M University–Kingsville.